T0145411

Techniques
in Prayer
Therapy

Techniques in Prayer Therapy

Joseph Murphy
Ph.D., D.D.

Published 2019 by Gildan Media LLC
aka G&D Media
www.GandDmedia.com

Design by Meghan Day Healey of Story Horse, LLC

Library of Congress Cataloging-in-Publication Data is available upon request

ISBN: 978-1-7225-0140-2

10   9   8   7   6   5   4   3   2   1

Contents

Introduction
Wonders Happen When You Pray

This book was written for the purpose of telling you how to reach the source of your good, and get desired results through praying effectively.

Do you know how to pray? How long is it since you prayed as part of your everyday activities? In an emergency, in time of danger or trouble, in illness, and when death lurks, prayers pour forth—your own and your friends. Just read your daily newspaper. It is reported that prayers are being offered up all over the nation for a child stricken with a so-called incurable ailment, for peace among nations, for a group of miners trapped in a flooded mine. Later it is reported that when rescued, the miners said that they prayed and sang while waiting for rescue; an airplane pilot says that he prayed as he made a successful emergency landing.

Certainly, prayer is an ever-present help in time of trouble; but you do not have to wait for trouble to make prayer an integral and constructive part of your life. The dramatic answers to prayer make headlines and are the subject of testimonies to the effectiveness of prayer. What of the many humble prayers of children, the simple thanksgiving of grace at the table daily, the faithful devotions wherein the individual seeks only communion with God?

My work with people has made it necessary for me to study the various approaches to prayer. I have experienced the power of prayer in my own life, and I have talked and worked with many people who also have enjoyed the help of prayer. The problem usually is how to tell others how to pray. Prayer is an intimate and personal communication. People who are in trouble have difficulty in thinking and acting reasonably. They need an easy formula to follow, an obviously workable pattern that is simple and specific. Often they must be led to approach the emergency.

The Bible admonishes us to pray without ceasing. You can make prayer a constant, constructive factor in your life. Prayer can bring success into your life, it can sustain health, it will enable you to be more helpful to others. The forces that make prayer effective are universal. It is not alone the technique or process of prayer that causes the Infinite Intelligence to respond, rather *it is according to our faith* (or complete mental acceptance) *that it is done unto us.* All of us tap the same Healing Principle. Of course, a technique based on an understanding of what we are doing and why we are doing it will help us to bring about a subjective embodiment of our desires. This is why I am going to suggest in this book techniques of prayer and formulas that have worked.

Emerson defined prayer as "the contemplation of the truths of life from the highest point of view." The Bible teaches us to devote our minds and attention to certain selected truths such as, *Whatsoever things are true, whatsoever things are lovely, whatsoever things are of good report; if there be any virtue, and if there be any praise, think on these things.* PHIL. 4:8. Essentially, answered prayer is the realization of your heart's desire.

Everybody prays because desire is prayer. All of us desire health, happiness, security, peace of mind, true expression, etc., but many fail to achieve clearly defined results. A university professor admitted to me recently, "I know if I changed my mental pattern and redirected my emotional life, my ulcers would not recur, but I do not have any technique, process, or *modus operandi*. My mind wanders back and forth on my many problems, and I feel frustrated, defeated, and unhappy." This professor had a desire for perfect health; he needed a knowledge of mental and spiritual laws which would enable him to fulfill his desire.

In this book techniques and formulas are given which will enable men to prove the age-old Biblical truth, *What things soever ye desire, when ye pray, believe that ye receive them, and ye shall have them.* MARK 11:24. Here Jesus states categorically, emphatically, and unequivocally that all we have to do is to believe; therefore the law behind answered prayer is the law of belief. This belief is not based on a particular creed, dogma, institution, organization, church, or person, but is based on a realization of a Universal Creative Law which sustains the world and all things therein contained.

To believe is to accept something as true. Whatever man's conscious, reasoning mind accepts as true engenders a corresponding reaction from his subconscious mind which is one with Infinite Intelligence and the Infinite Power of God. The subconscious mind works through the creative law which responds to the nature of man's thoughts bringing about conditions, experiences, and events in the image and likeness of his habitual thought-pattern, proving the truth stated so succinctly in the Bible: *As a man thinketh in his heart, so is he.*

It is not the thing believed in that brings an answer to man's prayer; the answer to prayer results when the individual's subconscious mind responds to the mental picture or thought in his mind. This law of belief is operating in all religions of the world and is the reason why they are psychologically true. The Buddhist, the Christian, the Moslem, and the Hebrew all may get answers to their prayers, not because of the particular creed, religion, affiliation, ritual, ceremony, formula, liturgy, incantation, sacrifices, or offerings, but solely because of belief or mental acceptance and receptivity about that for which they pray.

The law of life is the law of belief, and belief could be summed up briefly as a thought in your mind. As a man thinks, feels, believes so is the condition of his mind, body, and circumstances.

There is only One Creative Principle operating in the world. It is responsive to all men and is no respecter of persons. The nature of this Creative Principle is responsiveness. As you apply the simple techniques outlined in this book, you will discover a power within you which can lift you out of a state of frustration, illness, loneliness, discord, or poverty, and it can set you on the highroad to freedom, happiness, and radiant health. This Creative Intelligence existed before you and I were born, before any church or world existed; the great eternal truths of life antedate all religions. It is with these thoughts in mind that I urge you in the following chapters to lay hold of this wonderful, magical, healing, transforming power which will bind up mental and physical wounds, proclaim liberty to the fear-ridden mind, and liberate you completely from the limitations of poverty, failure, misery, lack, and confusion. All you have to do is to unite mentally and emotionally with this Creative Power, and let wonders happen when you pray.

1
Prayer Establishes Constructive Patterns

There is nothing difficult about prayer. Whoever reads this book and applies the principles set forth will be able to pray effectively for himself and others. True prayer utilizes the Universal Law of action and reaction. Thought is incipient action; the reaction is the response from a Deeper Mind which corresponds with the nature of the thought. Think good, good follows; think evil, evil follows.

When you pray, you are implanting a certain thought pattern or mental image in the Universal Creative Mind which accepts what you consciously believe to be true. The Creative Law knows exactly how to change thoughts into things and will begin to execute the thought patterns given to it; the effects will be observable as form, function, experience, or event.

The following are examples of effective prayer:

He Trusted In God

An article appeared in our local newspaper about a boy in the Korean War who miraculously was saved from what seemed certain death by repeating the verses of the 23rd Psalm. Bullets were whizzing past him, his buddies were all killed, his knees were shaking as he prayed aloud, "The Lord is my shepherd, I shall not want, He leadeth me beside the still waters, He restoreth my soul . . ." An inner peace and confidence welled up within him; he was not touched as he found his way to safety and freedom. Infinite Intelligence within him had responded to his prayer of faith and trust.

Thinking Of God

An elderly woman who listens regularly to a radio program I have conducted in Southern California for the past twelve years wrote to me saying that she had learned to pray through our Sunday morning prayer-therapy instruction. She stated that she had jotted down on a piece of paper all that she had been taught about God—God is Infinite Intelligence, Boundless Love, Omnipotence, Infinite Wisdom, Indescribable Beauty, Absolute Harmony, the Creative Intelligence which had formed and vitalized her body with all of its organs. Every morning and evening for five or ten minutes she would think quietly and with single-ness of interest on these qualities and attributes of God, silently claiming that these truths were being absorbed into her mentality. Within a month's time an entire tumorous growth had disappeared as proved by X-ray and physical examination by her physician.

This woman did not directly treat her tumorous growth which was the solidified effect of her previous thought patterns. As she filled her mind with state-ments of truth, a corresponding change took place in her body. She continued to "unthink" the nega-tive thoughts by thinking of God and His love which finally corrected the condition.

The Art Of Prayer

If you would become a master of the art of prayer, begin immediately to attach yourself mentally and emotion-ally to an idea, a plan, or a purpose; it will not be long before you will begin to experience physical evidence of the physical reaction to your thoughts. However do not discontinue your prayers with the first evidence of results. You must keep on praying with the conviction that you are operating a mental and spiritual Law which responds to your mental activity which maintains you in peace. Remember that any idea on which you meditate and feel as true incubates in your subconscious mind and is expressed in your life. To know what you are doing and why you are doing it will give you faith and confidence in your prayer life.

Prayer—A Change Of Mind

In prayer you experience a change of mind as you discover what the truth is, and your mind begins to conform to that truth. Prayer reveals the truth that God is Supreme and Omnipotent to solve all human problems. No matter what kind of difficulty may be facing you, no matter how complicated the situation may seem, prayer can bring about a harmonious resolution and rearrangement of your affairs in accord with divine order.

Prayer is not an act of asking God for anything; neither is prayer an effort to change the will of God. Prayer merely changes the conditions in your own mind. Prayer is not a timid suppliant, begging, beseeching approach to a God in space for a favor;

rather prayer is the positive effort of a man acting with a fervent belief and confidence that God, which is Infinite Intelligence, will respond according to the nature of the thoughts embodied in the mind. The answer to prayer is in man's own mind based on the truth, *According to your faith is it done unto you. Prayer Is the Practice of the Presence of God* in your life and all your affairs. It is a belief God is where you are and is speaking through you always.

You are praying whenever you are thinking of God and His Love and Wisdom and when you feel your oneness with God. Likewise you are praying whenever you are reading or meditating on the spiritual truths of the Bible or any other spiritual book.

Many people pray hundreds of times during the day by silently claiming as they go about their business that God is guiding, directing, and acting through them at all times, and that He watches over them in all their ways. Prayer is often referred to as *the practice of the Presence of God* which means that you realize that the Intelligence and Wisdom of God are working through you bringing about a harmonious solution where the trouble seems to be. This attitude of mind changes the difficulty into harmony. You can *practice the Presence of God* by doing everything from the standpoint of the Golden Rule and the Law of Love.

God Answers

Wise action will follow wise thoughts. A *wise thought* is to know that God or Infinite Intelligence is guiding you now, and that He knows the answer; therefore you affirm boldly that you know the answer. *Before they call, I will answer!* In praying for an answer to your problem it is foolish to neglect or overlook the obvious and common sense thing to do; take whatever practical steps that seem necessary. Claim divine guidance, and the steps you take will be dictated and governed by Divine Wisdom which is the dominant belief of your mind. In prayer you make contact through your thought with the Divine Presence which dwells within you, and having consciously done that, you call forth His Wisdom, Power, and Infinite Intelligence to resolve the various difficulties or troubles in your life, taking them in due order by solving the most pressing problems first. The right way to pray for the answer to all your problems is to feel and know that the Indwelling God knows only the answer; because this is true, you will know the answer and recall the truth; *He never faileth.*

Praying To God And What It Means

The Bible says, *God is a Spirit: and they that worship him must worship him in spirit and in truth.* JOHN

4:24. *To worship* means that you count worthy by giving supreme attention to something. This means that you are to give your supreme allegiance, loyalty, and devotion to the Spirit within, recognizing It as Supreme Power and the Cause and Substance of all things. Spirit is without face, form, or figure, time-less, shapeless, and ageless. The childish concept of a God as a grandfather in the skies, sitting on a celestial throne, must give way to the realization that God is Mind and Spirit within you which animates and sustains you. God is life. We do not see Life but we feel we are alive.

The good and evil we experience are simply due to our personal relationship through our thinking to the Life Principle which is forever Whole, Pure, and Perfect in Itself. Be sure not to give power to created things or effects; go to the cause of all, the Spirit within you. This Spirit or God is conditioned in your life according to the nature of your thought-life. There is only one Creative Principle and It is forever flowing through your habitual thought-patterns and imagery. This is why you make or create all experiences, events, and conditions of your life after your own image and likeness. This is the basis of all prayer whether we use this law consciously or unconsciously.

Do not be confused by the Biblical references "He" and "Him" denoting God. In ancient times the

Hebrew mystics used the word "It" when they were referring to God, but this has been discontinued as it seemed to lack the reverence and respect due to the Father of all. There are about seventysix or more names given to God in the Bible, but all these names represent qualities, attributes, characteristics, and potencies of God.

Assuming Certa In Postures, Etc .

In some parts of the world people practice rigid discipline of the body, breathing exercises, physical gymnastics, assuming peculiar and absurd postures. It is wholly unnecessary to bow down, genuflect, or prostrate yourself before the Creative Law.

This Principle of Life is no respecter of persons, we cannot cajole, bribe, or flatter it. It is Impersonal Law. All forms of physical gymnastics and postures are a waste of time and effort, and do not lead anywhere from the standpoint of building confidence in your prayer-life. The path to God is always and only through the mind and heart, not by way of the body. Prayer is effective because of the soul's sincere desire to unite with God and to reproduce His qualities and attributes right here and now so that like Job we can say, *And yet in my flesh do I see God.*

Thus in the wisdom of the universe, man establishes constructive patterns in his affairs and body by praying and aspiring to realize the perfection of God in his own life. This process is an instinctive or natural way of praying. The reverent man thinks right and acts in accord with the good impulses he engenders.

2
Techniques Of Prayer

When we come to analyze prayer, there are many different approaches or methods. We will not consider in this book the formal, ritual prayers used in religious services. These have an important place in group worship. We are immediately concerned with the methods of personal prayer for use in your daily life and in helping others.

Prayer is the formulation of an idea concerning something we wish to accomplish. Circumstances and individuals suggest different approaches, but all must establish a clear statement of the benefit, the healing, the purpose for which the prayer is offered.

The Visualization Technique

The easiest and most obvious way to formulate an idea is to visualize it, to see it in your mind's eye as vividly as if it were alive. We can see with the naked eye only what already exists in the external world; in a similar way what we can visualize in the mind's eye already exists in the invisible realms of our mind. Any picture which we have in the mind is the substance of things hoped for and the evidence of things not seen. What we form in our imagination is as real as any part of our body. The idea and the thought are real and will one day appear in our objective world if we are faithful to our mental image.

This process of thinking forms impressions on the mind; these impressions in turn become manifested or expressed on the screen of space as forms, functions, facts, and experiences. The builder visualizes the type of building he wants; he sees it as he desires it to be completed. His imagery and thought-processes become a plastic mold from which the building will emerge—a beautiful or an ugly one, a skyscraper or a very low one. His mental imagery is projected as it is drawn on paper; eventually the contractor and his workers gather the essential materials, and the building progresses until it stands finished, conforming perfectly to the mental patterns of the architect.

Visualization Technique For An Audience

Each Sunday I use the visualization technique prior to speaking from the platform. I quiet the wheels of my mind in order that I may present to the subconscious mind my images of thought; then I picture the entire auditorium and the seats filled with men and women, and each one of them illumined and inspired by the Healing Presence. I see them as radiant, happy, and free.

Having first built up the idea in my imagination, I quietly sustain it there as a mental picture while I imagine I hear men and women exclaiming aloud, "I am healed," "I feel wonderful," "I've had an instantaneous healing," "I'm transformed," etc. I keep this up for about ten minutes or more, knowing and feeling that each person is a tabernacle of God's Presence, and that Divine Love saturates each mind and body making them whole, pure, relaxed, and perfect. I see to the point where I actually can hear the imaginary voices of the multitudes proclaiming the glory of God; then I release the whole picture and go onto the platform. Almost every Sunday some people stop and say that their prayers were answered.

Mental Movie Method

The Chinese say, "A picture is worth a thousand words." William James, the father of American psychology, stressed the fact that the subconscious mind will bring to pass any picture held in the mind backed by faith. "Act as though I am, and I will be."

A number of years ago I was in the Middle West lecturing in several states and I desired to have a permanent location. One evening in a hotel in Spokane, Washington, I relaxed completely on the couch, immobilized my attention, and in a quiet, passive manner imagined that I was talking to a large audience, saying in effect, "I am glad to be here. I have prayed for this ideal church and opportunity." I saw in my mind's eye the imaginary audience and I felt the reality of it all. I played the role of the actor, dramatized this mental movie, and felt satisfied that this picture was being conveyed to my subconscious mind which would bring it to pass in its own way. The next morning on awakening I felt a great sense of peace and satisfaction, and in a few days' time I received a telegram asking me to take over a church in the East which I did, and enjoyed immensely for several years.

The method outlined here appeals to many who have described it as the "mental movie method." I have received numerous letters from people who listen to my radio lectures and Sunday morning talks, telling me of the wonderful results they get using this technique in the sale of their property. I suggest to those who have homes or property for sale that they satisfy themselves in their own mind that their price is right; then claim that Infinite Intelligence is attracting to them the buyer who really wants to have the property, and who will love it and prosper in it. After having done this I suggest that they quiet their mind, relax, let go, and get into a drowsy, sleepy state which reduces all mental effort to a minimum; then they are to picture the check in their hands, rejoice in the check, give thanks for the check, and go off to sleep feeling the naturalness of the whole mental movie created in their own mind. They must act as though it were an objective reality, and the subconscious mind will take it as an impression, and through the deeper currents of the mind the buyer and the seller are brought together. A mental picture held in the mind backed by faith will come to pass.

The Baudoin Technique

Charles Baudoin was a professor of Rousseau Institute in France. He was a brilliant psychotherapist, and a research director of the New Nancy School of Healing, who in 1910 taught that the best way to impress the subconscious mind was to enter into a drowsy, sleepy state, or a state akin to sleep, in which all effort was reduced to a minimum; then in a quiet, passive, receptive way, by reflection, convey the idea to the subconscious. The following is his formula: "A very simple way of securing this (impregnation of the subconscious mind) is to condense the idea which is to be the object of suggestion, to sum it up in a brief phrase which can be readily graven on the memory, and to repeat it over and over again as a lullaby."

Baudoin emphasized the fact that when we enter into "the state akin to sleep" (betwixt the waking and sleeping state), effort is reduced to a minimum, and we can focus our attention on our good with ease and without strain. We induce this state by feeling sleepy.

Innumerable experiments on persons have shown that the subconscious mind will accept any idea, suggestion, or mental picture which is felt as true by the conscious mind, and works out every suggestion to the minutest detail in the results which flow from it. The subconscious mind is entirely under the control of the conscious or objective mind. With the utmost fidelity it reproduces and manifests in the final consequences whatever the conscious mind impresses upon it.

The Practical Application
of Baudoin Technique

A lady in one of our classes last year was engaged in a prolonged, bitter family lawsuit over a will. Her husband had bequeathed his entire estate to her, and his sons and daughters were bitterly fighting to break the will. The Baudoin technique was outlined in detail to her, and this is what she did: She relaxed her body in an armchair, entered into the sleepy state, and as suggested, condensed the idea of her need into a phrase consisting of six words easily graven on the memory. "It is finished in Divine Order." The significance of these words to her meant that Infinite Intelligence operating through Law (the subconscious mind) would bring about a harmonious adjustment in Divine Order. She continued this procedure every night for about ten nights; after she got into a sleepy state she would affirm slowly, quietly, and feelingly the statement: "It is finished in Divine Order," over and over again, feeling a sense of inner peace and a letting go; then she went off into her deep, normal sleep.

On the morning of the eleventh day following the use of the above technique, she awakened with a sense of well-being, a conviction that it was finished.

Her attorney called her the same day, saying that the opposing attorney and his clients were willing to settle. A harmonious agreement was reached, and litigation was discontinued.

The Sleeping Technique

By entering into a sleepy, drowsy state, effort is reduced to a minimum. The conscious mind is submerged to a great extent when in a sleepy state. The reason for this is that the highest degree of outcropping of the subconscious occurs prior to sleep and just after we awaken. In this state the negative thoughts which tend to neutralize your desire and so prevent acceptance by the subconscious no longer present themselves.

The Sleeping Technique and Destructive Habits

Assume a comfortable posture, relax your body, and be still. Get into a sleepy state and in that sleepy state say quietly, over and over again as a lullaby, "I am completely free from this habit; sobriety and peace of mind reign supreme." Repeat the above slowly, quietly, and lovingly for five or ten minutes night and morning. Each time you repeat the above statement its emotional value becomes greater. When the urge comes, repeat the above formula out loud to yourself. By this means you induce the subconscious to accept the idea and a healing follows.

Solving Problems While You Sleep

During the course of an interview, a young man asked me how he could locate his father's will. His father had passed on and apparently had left no will. The young man's sister told him that their father had confided to her that a will had been executed which was fair to all. All attempts to locate the will had failed. I suggested he turn his request over to his subconscious mind at night before sleep. This is the method he followed: "I now turn this request over to the subconscious mind. It knows just where the will is. It reveals it to me." Then he condensed his request into one word, "Answer."

He repeated this prayer over and over again as a lullaby. He lulled himself to sleep for several nights with the word, "Answer." A few nights later he had a very vivid realistic dream. He saw the name and address of a certain bank. He went there and found a safe deposit vault registered in the name of his father. This was the answer to his prayer.

The Bible Technique

What things soever ye desire, when ye pray, believe that ye receive them, and ye shall have them. MARK 11:24. Note the difference in the tenses. The inspired writer tells us to believe and accept as true the fact that our desire *has already been* accomplished and fulfilled, that it is already completed, and that its realization *will follow* as a thing in the future.

The success of this technique depends on the confident conviction that the thought, the idea, the picture is already a fact in the mind, and in order for anything to have substance in the realm of the mind, it must be thought of as actually existing there.

Here in a few cryptic words is a concise and specific direction for making use of the creative power of thought by impressing upon the subconscious the particular thing which we desire. Your thought, idea, plan, or purpose is as real on its own plane as your hand or your heart. In following the Bible technique you completely eliminate from your mind all consideration of conditions, circumstances, or anything which might imply adverse contingencies. You are planting a seed (concept) in the mind which if you leave undisturbed will infallibly germinate into external fruition.

She Lost a Ring

I am writing this chapter at the beautiful Wishing Well, Rancho Santa Fe, a few hundred miles from Los Angeles. One of the guests lost a very valuable diamond. She had gone horseback-riding and discovered the loss when she returned. At my suggestion she prayed as follows: "Infinite Intelligence knows where the ring is. There can be no loss except I admit the loss in my mind, as all experiences come through my mind. I know Infinite Intelligence will now reveal the whereabouts of the ring to me. I see it on my finger, I feel it, and I know it is mine. I believe I have it now. I accept it mentally, for my thought is as real as the ring."

She quietly affirmed the above for a few minutes, and immediately afterwards she had an inner feeling or urge to drive back along one of the paths she had taken. Her horse stopped at the very spot where her ring was. The subjective mind operates throughout all nature, and in the horse, also. The ways of the subconscious mind are not always obvious. This incident illustrates the law of belief and the results which must inevitably follow.

Cause Of Failure To Get Results

Our failure to achieve the desired result always is due to our distrust in the law of growth. If we place a seed in the ground, it will grow. If we give up hope, fret, worry, and get anxious, we are actually denying the germinating power of the idea planted in our mind. Our doubt or fear is a thought in opposition to our desire, which if indulged in neutralizes the one first formed and results in its complete disintegration. We must keep out those negative thoughts of doubt and fear which only result in the opposite of what we are praying for. The law of belief as expounded and elaborated on in the Bible is to feel the pleasure and satisfaction in foreseeing the certain accomplishment of our desires.

The "Thank You" Technique

Paul recommends that we make known our requests to God with praise and thanksgiving. Some extraordinary results follow this simple method of prayer. The thankful heart is always close to the creative forces of the Universe, causing countless blessings to flow toward us by the law of reciprocal relationship based on a cosmic law of action and reaction.

A father promises his son a car for graduation; the boy has not yet received the car, but he is very thankful and happy, and is as joyous as though he had actually received the car. He knows his father will fulfill his promise, and is full of gratitude and joy even though he has not yet received the car, objectively speaking. He has, however, received it with joy and thankfulness in his mind. Oftentimes you have gone to a store and ordered a fur coat or hat, although they did not have exactly what you wanted. But you specified what you wanted and paid for it, and the clerk said they would send it. You thanked the clerk or owner and walked away without the coat or hat. You were absolutely sure of receiving the merchandise ordered in the near future because you trusted and believed in the integrity and honesty of the man who operated the business. How much more should we trust the Infinite and the Creative Law which never changes and responds with absolute fidelity to our trust and belief in It!

It Worked For Mr. Broke

I shall illustrate how Mr. Broke applied this technique with excellent results. He said, "Bills are piling up, I am out of work, I have three children and no money. What shall I do?" Regularly every night and morning for a period of about three weeks he repeated the words, "Thank you, Father, for the Law of Opulence," in a relaxed, peaceful manner until the feeling or mood of thankfulness dominated his mind. He imagined he was addressing the Infinite, knowing, of course, that he could not see God. He was seeing with the inner eye of spiritual perception, realizing that his thought-image of wealth was the *first cause* relative to the money, position, and food he needed. His thought-feeling was the substance of wealth untrammeled by antecedent conditions of any kind. By repeating, "Thank you, Father," over and over again, his mind and heart were lifted up to the point of acceptance, and when fear, thoughts of lack, poverty, and distress came into his mind, he would say, "Thank you, Father," as often as necessary. He knew that as he kept up this *thankful attitude* he would recondition his mind to the idea of wealth, which is what happened. Mr. Broke met on the street a former employer of his whom he had not seen for twenty years; the man offered him a very lucrative position and advanced him $500.00 as a temporary loan. Today Mr. Broke is vice president of the corporation for which he works. His recent remark to me was, "I shall never forget the wonders of 'Thank you, Father.' It has worked wonders for me."

Why His Technique Worked

All material things *must* have their origin in the Invisible or Spirit; all of creation is evidence of thought-images and ideas in the Mind of God which became form according to the Creative Law. There is only one Creative Process, and man through his thoughts sets in motion the Creative Law. We may be using it consciously or unconsciously; nevertheless we are always using the Creative Law for the simple reason that we are *always* impressing some sort of ideas and mental pictures upon It, whether we are aware of it or not. All our existing limitations result from our having habitually impressed upon our subconscious mind ideas of limitation, restriction, and bondage of all kinds. When we realize that our conditions and circumstances are never real *causes* in themselves, but only the result of prior thinking, we reverse our method of thinking and regard our ideal as real, and as we mentally and emotionally unite with the ideal in our mind, we change the outer manifestations to agree with the inner thought-images and thus change our world.

Affirmative Method

The effectiveness of affirmation lies in its intelligent application of definite and specific positives. For example, a boy adds three and three and puts down seven on the blackboard. The teacher affirms with mathematical certainty that three and three are six; therefore the boy changes his figures accordingly. Likewise when we affirm the Truth about a person, we must conform to the Principles of Truth regardless of appearances. The power of the affirmation process depends on the faith and understanding of the person affirming.

The Affirmative Method
Heals Acute Gallbladder Trouble

This method was chosen by the writer for use on his sister, who was to be operated on for the removal of gallstones, based on the diagnosis of hospital tests and the usual X-ray procedures. She asked me to pray for her. We are separated geographically about 6,500 miles, but there is no time or space in Mind. Spirit or Mind is present in its entirety at every point simultaneously. In prayer treatment for another, you withdraw all thought from the contemplation of symptoms and from the corporeal personality altogether, and think of the individual as pure spirit and expressing the vitality, wholeness, beauty and perfection of that Spirit. I affirmed as follows: "This prayer treatment is for my sister Kate. She is relaxed and at peace, poised, balanced, serene, and calm. Her mind and spirit are the Mind and Spirit of God. The Healing Intelligence which created her body is now transforming every cell, nerve, tissue, muscle, and bone of her being into God's Perfect Pattern. Silently, quietly, all distorted thought patterns are removed and dissolved, and the vitality, wholeness, and beauty of the Spirit are made manifest in every atom of her being. She is now open and receptive to this Healing Presence which flows through her like a river, restoring her to perfect health, harmony, and peace. All distortions and ugly thought images are now washed away by the Infinite Ocean of Love and Peace flowing through her, and it is so."

I affirmed the above several times a day, and at the end of two weeks my sister had an examination which showed a remarkable healing, and the X-rays proved negative.

To *affirm* is to state that it is so, and as you maintain this attitude of mind as true, regardless of all evidence to the contrary, you will receive an answer to your prayer. Your thought can only affirm, for even if you deny something you are actually affirming the presence of what you deny. Repeating an affirmation, knowing what you are saying and why you are saying it, leads the mind to that state of consciousness where it accepts that which you state as true. Keep on affirming the Truth until you get the subconscious reaction which satisfies.

The Argumentative Technique
In brief, the argumentative method consists of spiritual reasoning, where you convince yourself that the

patient is a victim of false beliefs and groundless fears, and that the disease or ailment is due only to a distorted, twisted pattern of thought which has taken form in his body; this wrong belief in some external power and external causes has now externalized as sickness and can be changed through a knowledge of the Law, which shows there is only One Primary Cause—Living Spirit or God, and Spirit can't be sick, frustrated, or unhappy. Spirit is unconditioned, not hampered by conditions of any sort, and is not subject to illness.

The basis of all healing is a change of belief. You reason out in your mind that the Infinite Intelligence created the body and all its organs; therefore It knows how to heal it, can heal it, and is doing so now as you speak. You argue in the courtroom of your mind that the disease is a shadow of the mind, based on disease-soaked, morbid thought-imagery. You continue to build up all the evidence you can muster on behalf of the Power of the Healing Presence which created all the organs in the first place and has a perfect pattern of every cell, nerve, and tissue within It; then you render a verdict in the courthouse of your mind in favor of your patient. You liberate the sick one by faith and spiritual understanding. Your mental and spiritual evidence is overwhelming; there being but One Mind, what you feel as true will be resurrected in the experience of the other. There is but One Mind common to all individual men.

She Won The Argument

Recently a listener of our radio programs in Los Angeles prayed for her mother in New York City who had a coronary thrombosis. She prayed as follows: "God is the only Presence and the only Power, the only Living Reality, the Living Spirit Almighty. This Presence and Power is right where my mother is. God is her Life, and that Life is her Life now. The bodily condition is but a reflection of her thought-life, like shadows cast on the screen. I know that in order to change the images on the screen, I must change the projection reel. My mind is the projection reel, and I now project in my own mind the image of wholeness, harmony, and perfect health for my mother. The Infinite Healing Presence which created my mother's body and all her organs is now saturating every atom of her being, and His River of Peace flows through every cell of her being. The doctors are divinely guided and directed, and whoever touches my mother is governed over by the Overshadowing Presence. I know that disease has no ultimate reality; if it had, no one could be healed. I now align myself with the Infinite Principle of Love and Life, and I know and decree that harmony, health, and peace are now being expressed in my mother's body. There is no power to challenge Omnipotence. The Healing Presence of God is now flowing through her. It is wonderful!"

Her mother had a most remarkable recovery after a few days, much to the amazement of the specialist who complimented her on her faith in God. The argumentative method of prayer on the part of her daughter produced certain conclusions in her mind and set the Creative Law of Mind in motion on the subjective side of life, which manifested through her mother's body as perfect health and harmony. There is only One Mind, and what the daughter felt as true about her mother was simultaneously resurrected in the experience of the mother.

The Absolute Method

The person practicing this form of prayer treatment mentions the name of the patient, such as John Jones; then quietly and silently thinks of God and His qualities and attributes, such as God is All Bliss, Boundless Love, Infinite Intelligence, All Peaceful, Boundless Wisdom, Absolute Harmony, and Indescribable Beauty and Perfection. As he quietly thinks along these lines, he is lifted up in consciousness into a new spiritual wave length, at which time he feels that the Infinite Ocean of God's Love is now dissolving everything unlike Itself in the mind and body of John Jones for whom he is praying. He feels all the Power and Love of the Godhead is now focused on John Jones, and whatever is bothering or vexing him now is completely dissolved in the Presence of the Infinite Ocean of God's Love.

Modern Sound Wave Therapy

The absolute method of prayer might be likened to the sound wave or sonic therapy recently shown me by a distinguished physician in Los Angeles. He has an ultra sound wave machine which oscillates at a tremendous speed and sends sound waves to any area of the body to which it is directed. These sound waves can be controlled, and he told me of remarkable results in dissolving arthritic calcareous deposits and the healing and removal of other disturbing conditions.

To the degree that we rise in consciousness by contemplating the qualities and attributes of God, do we generate spiritual electronic waves of harmony, health, and peace. Many instantaneous healings follow the absolute method of prayer.

A Cripple Walks

Dr. Phineas Parkhurst Quimby, of whom we spoke previously, used the absolute method almost exclusively in the latter years of his healing career. He was really the father of psychosomatic medicine and the first psychoanalyst. He had the capacity to diagnose clairvoyantly the cause of the patient's troubles, pains, and aches. Quimby would tell the patient where the pain was and the cause behind it. In order to cure him Quimby said, "I must go to Him who sent me, and there I will contemplate your Divine Perfection; if I succeed, you will be healed." The phrase, "I must go to Him who sent me," is taken from the Bible. *Yet a little while I am with you, and then I go unto Him who sent me, You shall seek me and shall not find me: and where I am, thither you cannot come.* JOHN 7:33, 34. You will see the wonderful meaning of this as we proceed.

Quimby was called on to visit a woman who was lame, aged, and practically bedridden. He states that her ailment was due to the fact that she was imprisoned by a creed so small and contracted that she could not stand upright or move about. She was living in the tomb of fear and ignorance; furthermore she was taking the Bible literally and it frightened her. "In this tomb," Quimby said, "was the Presence and Power of God trying to burst the bars, break through the bonds, and rise from the dead." When she would ask others for an explanation of some passage of the Bible, the answer would be a stone; then she would hunger for the bread of life. Dr. Quimby diagnosed her case as a mind cloudy and stagnated due to excitation and fear caused by the inability to see clearly the meaning of the Scriptural passages she had been reading. This showed itself in the body by her heavy and sluggish feeling which would terminate in paralysis.

At this point Quimby asked her what was meant, *A little while I am with you and then I go to Him that sent me.* She replied that it meant Jesus went to heaven. Quimby explained what it really meant by telling her that *being with her a little while* meant his explanation of her symptoms, feelings, and their cause; *i.e.,* he had compassion and sympathy for her momentarily, but he could not remain in that mental state. The next step was *to go to Him that sent us,* which is the Presence of God in all of us.

Quimby immediately traveled in his mind and contemplated the Divine Ideal; i.e., the Vitality, Intelligence, Harmony, and Power of God functioning in the sick person. This is why he said to the woman, "Therefore where I go, you cannot come for you are in your narrow, restricted belief, and I am in health." This prayer and explanation produced an instantaneous sensation, and a change came over her mind. She walked without her crutches! She was as it were dead in error, and to bring her to life or truth was to raise her from the dead. "I quoted the resurrection of Christ and applied it to her own Christ or health; it produced a powerful effect on her." (*Quimby's Manuscripts*).

The Decree Method

> *Thou shalt also decree a thing, and it shall be established unto thee: and the light shall shine upon thy ways.*   JOB 22:28.

Power goes into our word according to the feeling and faith behind it. When we realize the Power that moves the world is moving on our behalf and is backing up our word, our confidence and assurance grow. We do not try to add power to Power; therefore there must be no mental striving, coercion, force, or mental wrestling.

A young girl used the decree method on a young man who was constantly phoning her, pressing her for dates, and meeting her at her place of business; she found it very difficult to get rid of him. She decreed as follows: "I release _____ unto God. He is in his true place at all times. I am free, and he is free. I now release this word into the Ocean of Infinite

Mind which is the Mind of the Almighty. Infinite Mind is the Only Power operating and It brings this to pass. I have decreed this, and it shall come to pass. It is so." She said he vanished and she has never seen him since, adding, "It was as though the ground swallowed him up."

How A Minister Got A Car

A young, struggling minister recently told me that he read the above-mentioned verse in the Bible, *Thou shalt also decree a thing* . . . He decreed as follows: "I am one with all the automobiles in the world. They are all God's ideas made manifest. I decree that Infinite Mind through the Law of Right Action reveals to me the ideal car suitable for my work. I trust the Deeper Mind implicitly. It knows how to bring it to pass in Its own way."

The sequel to this decree was most interesting. Secretly members of his congregation collected a sum of money and presented him with a new Chevrolet car after his church service. They said, "We have a surprise for you!" He was not surprised, because he knew the Deeper Mind has ways we know not of. The Infinite Intelligence acted on their mind causing them to fulfill what the minister had accepted as true in his own mind.

You can never know *how* your prayer will be answered. Man must never say, "I don't have the money to buy a car; therefore I must do without it." He can decree what he wants, and Infinite Mind will bring it to pass.

3

Practicing Prayer Therapy

Spiritual Healing And Faith Healing

True spiritual healing requires serious thought and consideration on the part of the person who undertakes it. Spiritual healing is not the same as faith healing. A faith healer is one who heals without any scientific understanding of the powers involved. He may claim that he has a special gift of healing, and the sick person's blind belief in him or his powers may bring results. Spiritual therapy is the synchronized, harmonious, and intelligent function of the conscious and subconscious levels of mind specifically directed for a definite purpose. The spiritual therapist must know what he is doing and why he is doing it. He trusts the law of healing. The voodoo doctor in South

Africa may heal by incantations, or a person may be healed by touching the so-called bones of saints or anything else which causes the patients to honestly believe in the method or process.

One Healing Principle

The subject of spiritual healing is creating a widespread interest all over the world at the present time. Man is gradually awakening to the healing powers resident in the subconscious mind. It is a well-known fact that all of the various schools of healing effect cures. The answer to all of this is that there is one universal healing principle, the subconscious mind, and one process of healing which is faith. That is why Paracelsus stated this great truth, "Whether the object of your faith be real or false, you will nevertheless obtain the same effects."

It is an established fact that cures have taken place in various shrines throughout the world, in Japan, India, Europe, and on the American continent. You will find many widely differing theories, each presenting indubitable evidences of healing. Obviously, to the thinker there must be some underlying principle common to them all. Regardless of the geographical location or the means used, there is only one healing principle, and the process of every healing is faith.

The first thing to remember is the dual nature of your mind. The subconscious mind is constantly amenable to the power of thought; furthermore, the subconscious mind has complete control of your body. We realize that remarkable healings take place through osteopathy, chiropractics, medicine, and naturopathy, as well as through the ministrations of the various churches, but we maintain that all of these healings are brought about through the subconscious mind—the only healer there is.

Subconscious Mind And Health

Notice how the subconscious mind heals a cut on your face caused by shaving; it knows exactly how to do it. The doctor dresses the wound and says, "Nature heals it." Nature refers to natural law, the law of the subconscious mind. The instinct of self-preservation is the first law of nature; your strongest instinct is the most potent of all auto-suggestions.

The Body Acts As It Is Acted On

It is a well-known fact that the symptoms of almost any disease can be induced in hypnotic subjects by suggestion. Disease can be artificially induced in your own body or that of another through suggestion in defiance of your natural instincts. It is perfectly natural and obvious that suggestions in harmony with instinctive autosuggestion would have greater power.

It is easier to maintain and restore health than it is to bring about sickness in the body. The faith that brings about healing is a certain mental attitude, a way of thinking, an inner certitude, an expectancy of the best.

Any method, technique, or process you may use which will bring about a change in the mind, or inspire a new mental atmosphere is legitimate; results will follow. Healing is due to a changed mental attitude, or to a transformation of the mind.

Blind Faith

Any method which causes you to move from fear and worry to faith and expectancy will heal. True, scientific, mental healing is brought about by the combined function of the conscious and subconscious mind scientifically directed. There are a great number who claim that because their theory produces results, it is, therefore, the correct one; this is as explained in this chapter, cannot be true.

You know there are many types of healing. Mesmer and others healed by claiming that they were sending forth a certain magnetic fluid; other men came along and said all this was nonsense, that the healing was due to suggestion. If you believe in the bones of saints to heal, or if you believe in the healing power of certain waters, you will get results because of the powerful suggestion given to your subconscious mind; it is the latter that does he healing. The witch doctor with his incantations also heals by faith.

All groups, psychiatrists, psychologists osteopaths, physicians, and churches, are using the one universal healing power resident in the subconscious mind. Each may proclaim that the healings are due to its theory. The process of all healing is a definite, positive, mental attitude, an inner certitude, or a way of thinking called *faith*. Healing is due to a confident expectancy which acts as a powerful suggestion to the subconscious mind releasing its healing potency.

One man does not heal by a power different from another. It is true he may have his own theory and method. There is only one healing power, your subconscious mind. Select the theory and method which you prefer. You can rest assured if you have the faith, you will get results.

Prayer Therapy At Redlands University

In the Los Angeles Examiner several years ago, John McDowell described tests being conducted in prayer therapy at Redlands University under the title "Psycho-somatic Tests Bare Prayer's Power." He writes as follows:

"Dr. William R. Parker, 37-year-old director of the clinic, today revealed for the first time that early results of prayer therapy in a group of twenty arthritic, tubercular, ulcer, and speech impediment patients have been favorable.

"These patients, who agreed to practice prayer therapy in addition to the university clinic's regular group psychological therapy, have been making greater progress than the clinic's regular patients," Dr. Parker said.

"For example: A stomach ulcer patient, relying solely on prayer and group therapy, has reported that for the last three weeks, all symptoms of his ailment have disappeared.

A Redlands University professor, afflicted most of his life with a severe case of stuttering which years of various treatments failed to correct, today has no trace of speech impediment after six months of prayer therapy.

"Another teacher, forced into retirement a year ago because of tuberculosis, is now back at his teaching job, apparently cured.

"'This man's doctor,—a tuberculosis specialist—recently gave him a sputum test,' Dr. Parker said. 'The test turned up negative, and the doctor was certain a mistake had been made. He immediately made another test, and that was negative too.'"

"Dr. Parker—a doctor of psychology, not medicine—stresses that prayer therapy is no 'quackish' miracle cure-all, but a scientific approach to prayer and its effect on the subconscious mind.

"The subconscious mind in the eyes of the still-pioneering psychosomatic medicine world is the fountainhead of many of mankind's afflictions, including arthritis, asthma, hay fever, multiple sclerosis, tuberculosis, ulcers, and high blood pressure.

"The psychomatic theory—hotly disputed by the medical profession—is that such ailments start as functional disorders in the subconscious and develop into organic disease, which doctors treat by attacking the symptoms rather than the cause.

"Prayer therapy according to Dr. Parker is a psychosomatic attempt to attack the causes of these disorders in the subconscious.

"'Four basic personality difficulties are at the root of everything that goes wrong in the subconscious mind,' Dr. Parker said. 'They are fear, hate, guilt, and inferiority.'

"In the Redlands prayer-therapy experiments these basic difficulties are first ferreted out through a series of standard psychological tests given to patients participating in the project.

"Subsequently, the patients meet in a ninety-minute group session once a week to discuss their problems. At these meetings each patient is given a sealed envelope containing information on one detrimental aspect of his or her personality uncovered in the tests.

"Once at home the patients open the envelopes, learn a new, undesirable phase of their personality, and resolve that particular difficulty in prayer daily until the next group meeting.

"There is only one 'must.' Each patient is required to pray regularly each night before he or she retires.

"'We insist on a prayer at that time, because the last thing that a person is thinking before going to sleep is most likely to penetrate to the subconscious,' Dr. Parker said.

"Dr. Parker, who first tried out his prayer theories himself during an onset of ulcers three years ago, said most of the patients have to be taught how to pray.

"The clinic's prayer-therapy patients are taught a positive approach to prayer, stressing love, and an uplifting concept of God and the universe.

"Our prayers are not a begging for health, but

are affirmations of the healing of the unhealthy element the patient wants to attack stated in such a positive, repetitious manner that eventually it sinks into the subconscious and becomes a part of that person,' Dr. Parker said.

"'In that manner, through prayer, destructive aspects within the subconscious can be attacked and eventually overcome, thus eliminating the basic causes of their physical ills.'"

Dr. Parker has written a book called *Prayer Can Change Your Life* which explains his remarkable and marvelous results in prayer therapy at Redlands University. He has also given several series of immensely popular class-lessons with me at the Wilshire Ebell Theater, Los Angeles, which created widespread interest to students of all religious affiliations. We had over twelve hundred registered students in one of our special classes on prayer therapy.

How To Heal Through Prayer Therapy
THE USUAL PROCEDURE IS AS FOLLOWS:
1. Take a look at the problem.
2. Then turn to the solution or way out known only to the subconscious mind.
3. Rest in a sense of deep conviction that it is done.

Do not weaken your treatment by saying, "I hope so!" or "It will be better!" The cellular set-up of your body will follow faithfully and honestly whatever blueprint the conscious mind hands over to it by way of the subconscious mind sometimes called the subjective or involuntary mind. Your feeling about the work to be done is "the boss." Know that health is yours! Harmony is yours! Become intelligent by becoming a vehicle for the infinite healing power of the subconscious mind. The reasons of failure are: Lack of confidence and too much effort. Pass on the idea of health to the subconscious mind to the point of conviction; then relax. Get yourself off of your hands. Say to conditions and circumstances, "This, too, shall pass." Through relaxation you impress the subconscious mind enabling the kinetic energy behind the idea to take over and bring it into concrete realization.

The Tendency of the Subconscious is Lifeward

The body of man portrays the workings of his inner mind. Our real powers are resident in the subconscious mind. No one knows all of the workings of the subconscious mind for it is infinite in its scope. We learn what we can about how it works; then we use it accordingly. There is an intelligence which will take care of the body if we let it alone. The conscious mind always interferes with its fivesense-evidence based on outer appearances, leading to the sway of false beliefs, fears, and opinion. When fear, false beliefs, and negative patterns are made to register in the subconscious mind through psychological, emotional conditioning, there is no other course open to the subconscious mind except to act on the blueprint specification offered to it.

The subjective self within you works continuously for the general good, reflecting an innate principle of harmony behind all things. Study the works of Edison, Carver, Einstein, and many others who, without too much education, knew how to tap the subconscious mind for its manifold treasures. Have a reason for faith in yourself. You cannot get very far if you do not believe in what you do not see. I do not see love, but I feel it; I do not see beauty, but I see its manifestations. Our greatest failing is a lack of confidence in the powers of the subconscious mind. Get acquainted with your inner powers. Of what use is it to know in principle that you are perfect if you cannot bring it out? Self-realization, plus feeling, is the only key to healing. Know your mind, and how to use it.

Easy Does It!

A house-owner once remonstrated with a furnace repairman for charging two hundred dollars for fixing the boiler. The mechanic said, "I charged five cents for the missing bolt, and one hundred and ninety-nine dollars and ninety-five cents for knowing what was wrong."

Similarly, your subconscious mind is the master-mechanic, the all-wise one, who knows ways and means of healing any organ of your body, as well as your affairs. Decree health, and the subconscious mind will establish it; but relaxation is the key. "Easy does it." Do not be concerned with details and means, but know the end result. Get the *feel* of the happy solution of your problem, whether it is health, finances, or employment. Remember how you felt after you had recovered from a severe state of illness. Bear in mind that the feeling is the touchstone of all subconscious demonstration. Your new idea must be felt subjectively in a finished state—not in the future—but as *now* coming about.

Taking God's Pattern

The following is a prayer for perfect health. A minister I knew in South Africa applied this prayer and healed himself. Several times a day he would affirm slowly and quietly, first making certain he was completely relaxed mentally and physically, "The perfection of God is now being expressed through me. The idea of health is now filling my subconscious mind. The image God has of me is a perfect image, and my subconscious mind recreates my body in perfect accordance with the perfect image held in the mind of God."

This is a simple, easy way of conveying the idea of perfect health to your subconscious mind. In prayer therapy or spiritual healing our only tool is spiritual thought.

Impressing The Subconscious Mind

A wonderful way to impress the subconscious mind is through disciplined or scientific imagination. The subconscious mind is the builder of the body and controls all its vital functions. I told a man suffering from functional paralysis to make a vivid picture of himself walking around in his office, touching the desk, answering the telephone, and doing all the things he ordinarily would do if he were healed. He lived the role and actually felt himself back in the office. I explained to him that as he imagined clearly the fulfillment of his desire, he was giving the subconscious mind something definite to work upon. The subconscious mind is the film upon which the picture is impressed. The subconscious mind develops the picture and objectifies it as an experience, condition, or event. One day after several weeks of frequent conditioning of the mind with this mental picture, by prearrangement the telephone range and kept ringing while his wife and nurse were out. The telephone was about twelve feet away, but he managed to answer the telephone. His wife knew he was healed at that hour. The healing power flowed to the focal point of his attention, and a healing followed. Psychologically speaking, the mental picture was developed in the dark house of his mind, and a complete healing followed. This man had a mental block which prevented impulses from the brain reaching his legs: therefore he said he could not walk. When he shifted his attention to the healing power within him, the power flowed through his focused attention enabling him to walk. The Bible says, "Whatsoever ye shall ask in prayer, believing, ye shall receive." To believe is to accept something as true, or to live in the state of being it; as you sustain this mood, you shall experience the joy of the answered prayer!

Pott's Disease Cured

I read an article which appeared in the magazine *Nautilus* some years ago about a boy suffering from Pott's disease, or tuberculosis of the spine, who had a remarkable healing. His name was Frederick Elias Andrews of Indianapolis, now minister of Unity School of Christianity, Kansas City, Missouri. His physician had pronounced him incurable. He began to pray, and from a crooked, twisted cripple going about on hands and knees, he became a strong, straight, well-formed man. He created his own affirmation, mentally absorbing the qualities he needed. He affirmed over and over again many times a day, "I am whole, perfect, strong, powerful, loving, harmonious, and happy." He persevered and said that this prayer was the last thing on his lips at night and the first thing in the morning. He prayed for others also by sending out thoughts of love and health. This attitude of mind and way of prayer returned to him multiplied. His faith and perseverance paid off big dividends. When thoughts of fear, anger, jealousy, or worry came into his mind, he would start his affirmation going in his mind. His subconscious mind responded according to the nature of his habitual thinking. This is the meaning of the statement in the Bible, "Go thy way, thy faith hath made thee whole."

4

How Prayer Works

Why No One Can Upset You

Many of you have heard these expressions frequently: "I'm deeply hurt, I can't get over it; I've been wounded to the quick; this is the last straw; I could forgive anything but not this." The only creative power is our own thought; consequently we are hurt by our own thoughts, by the movement of our own mind. Each individual has the power to react positively or negatively. It is not what the other person says or does that hurts you; it is your reaction to what is said or done. The suggestions and statements of others cannot create circumstances for us unless we accept these suggestions and give them mental consent; this process requires a movement of your own mind which, in the final analysis, is the only creative medium. You can think constructively or negatively, as you wish. You are free to choose how you will think and react.

The Case Of The Crystal-Gazer

One of the countries in which I have lived is India. A relative there told me about a friend of his who had gone to a crystal-gazer who told him that he had a bad heart and would die at the next new moon. It happened just as predicted. My relative also told me that this crystal-gazer was believed to have some strange occult powers and could do good or harm to a person. I suppose many of us have heard similar stupid, ridiculous, superstitious stories.

Let us look at what happened in the light of our knowledge of the way the subconscious mind works. Whatever the conscious, reasoning mind of man believes, the subconscious mind will accept and act upon. This is why the Bible says, "As a man man thinketh in his heart (subconscious mind), so is he," or "It is done unto us as we believe." In other words, the things we believe cause all our experiences. My relative's friend was happy, healthy, vigorous, and robust when he went to see the fortuneteller. She gave him a very negative prediction which acted like a posthypnotic suggestion. He became terrified and constantly dwelt upon the fact that he was going to die at the next new moon. He proceeded to tell everybody about it and got ready for the end. The activity took place in his own mind, and his own thought was the cause. He brought about his own so-called death, or rather destruction of the physical body, by his fear and expectation of the end.

The woman who predicted his death had no more power than the stones or sticks in the field. Her suggestion had no power to create or bring about the end she suggested. If he had known the laws of his mind, he would have completely rejected the negative suggestion and refused to give her word any attention, knowing in his heart that he was governed and controlled by his own thought and feeling. Like tin arrows aimed at a battleship, her prophecy could have been completely neutralized and dissipated without harming anyone. The suggestions of others in themselves have absolutely no power whatever over you except the power that you give them through your thoughts. You have to give your mental consent; you have to entertain the thought; then it becomes *your thought*, and you do the thinking. Remember, you have the capacity to choose. Choose life! Choose love! Choose health!

What It Means To Think

To think implies comparison of one thing with another, of one proposition with another. If the mental instrument of man can only say, "Yes," comparison is obviously impossible. To think is to choose. *Choose ye this day whom ye shall serve.* You have a choice between two things; to one of them you say, "Yes," to the other, "No."

For example, when you ask, "Why," you are seeking a reason. All reasoning involves selecting one thing and rejecting another. It would be impossible to select or reject unless your mind had the power of affirmation and rejecting. You are truly thinking when your thoughts are positive, constructive, harmonious, and when you reject all fears and contemplate the reality of your desire, knowing that there is an Almighty Power lodged in your subconscious depths which responds to your thought, and this Power will bring your thoughts to fruition. You are truly thinking when you reason things out in your mind, rejecting all concepts unfit for a mind dedicated to peace and harmony. You are truly thinking when you realize that there is a solution, a way out, knowing that a subjective wisdom will respond to your creative thoughts when you are free from fear. If you are worried, fearful, or anxious, you are not thinking in the true sense of the word; it is the race mind thinking in you. Think on whatsoever things are lovely and of good report.

How She Recouped Her Loss

A businesswoman in Los Angeles told me that she had attracted a charlatan who swindled her out of nearly fifteen thousand dollars. She became embittered, revengeful, hostile, and hateful toward all men and developed a martyr complex. She said that her misfortune was all due to bad luck. It was explained to her that her so-called misfortune was the silent unfolding of the bad thoughts of gloom and despondency which she had sowed in her deeper mind. What we sow, we reap, and our destiny depends on our choice of thoughts. The future is always the present grown up. We must remember that we are sowing seeds of thought in the garden of our mind every time we think. The good and bad seeds (thoughts) we deposit in our garden (mind) grow like the wheat and the tares until the harvest.

This woman admitted that she had been in a depressed and dejected state at the time she had attracted the confidence man. She was also quick to realize that her mood of despondency, grief, and self-pity, being a mood of loss, attracted to her someone who testified to her mental attitude of loss. Loss can come in many ways, and in her case it was a loss of joy, health, peace of mind, as well as money. This man could not have cheated her unless she had planted in the soil of her mind the seeds of loss, lack, and limitation. The law of cause and effect is always operating to bring in the results of our choice.

This person overcame her mental anxiety and sense of loss by using the following prayer two or three times a day: "I know there is nothing lost in Infinite Mind; all things subsist in the One Mind. I know that whatever I accept and believe in my mind, I experience. I positively refuse to accept the loss of my wealth. I choose mentally and emotionally to identify myself with my wealth, and it comes to me in avalanches of abundance. I know definitely, positively, and absolutely that I cannot experience anything except through my mental acceptance and belief. I accept wealth and abundance now. I wish for everyone what I wish for myself, for I know that love is the fulfilling of the law of health, wealth, and peace of mind."

As she repeated this prayer frequently, she reconditioned her mind to wealth. Whenever the thought of the swindler re-entered her mind, instead of reacting negatively she said, "I wish him well." This meant that she wished for him all the blessings of health, wealth, happiness, and peace of mind. After a few weeks she was in an exalted frame of mind. She took a position as private secretary to a stock broker, and in a few months time she made ten times as much as she had lost. Through information on the movement of certain stocks the deeper mind recovered her loss for her. A knowledge of the laws of our mind is the truth which sets us free.

Getting Back On The Beam

I knew a woman who hated her sister because the latter called her a slimy snake. She brooded over it for months, felt deeply hurt, and developed colitis as a result—all because of a few words uttered by her sister. She had to heal herself. In order to do this it was necessary for her to understand how her mind worked. The first thing she had to perceive was that the words uttered by her sister had absolutely no power whatsoever to affect her, as the only creative power was her own thought. A word is a thought expressed. The words which were thoughts expressed by her sister had no power to disturb her. They were not creative except as she entertained them in her own mind and reacted negatively. She had yielded to the thought of resentment; that thought then generated a negative emotion, followed by the objective manifestation in her colon. All three steps thought, emotion, and manifestation took place in her own mind. *It is not what people say and do that hurts us, it is our reaction and response.* In other words, the good and evil we experience are simply movements of our mind. The doctor told this woman that her ulcerative colitis was due to an emotional upheaval and he advised her to become loving and forgiving.

This is how she got back on the beam: She radiated thoughts of love, peace, and good will to her sister frequently during the day by affirming as follows, "I sincerely wish for my sister peace, health, and happiness, and I know that God's river of peace and love flow through her now and forevermore." This changed mental attitude on her part released the Infinite Healing Power which is within all, and in a few weeks' time she was completely whole, and all tests were negative.

The Healing Of An Ulcer

Mr. Jones had feelings of strong resentment, hostility, and anxiety. He said to me, "The doctor says I have a peptic ulcer. Do you think my resentment caused it?" In our discussion I discovered he was really suffering from an emotional reaction toward a business associate. It seems that his associate had ridiculed his suggestions at one of the board meetings, and he had been brooding over the ridicule at length. Our emotions, when suppressed, must find an outlet in disease such as ulcers, migraine, arthritis. Mr. Jones allowed this man to rob him of inner peace, health, joy, and mental efficiency.

The healing process he followed was to see clearly that he had to cremate, burn up, destroy, and annihilate ruthlessly all the negative thoughts in his mind which were causing the trouble. He realized that his business associate had no power to irritate, annoy, or disturb him. He said to me, "I shall never again in the whole course of my life give to others the prerogative or capacity to hurt me. I know now they do not possess any such power." This statement coming from him was, as you can readily see, fifty-one percent of the healing process; the rest was easy. He knew he had been entertaining mental gangsters, murderers, assassins, and marauders which robbed him of peace, tranquillity, and inner peace. His negative, destructive thoughts produced his peptic ulcer. His thoughts were the thieves who robbed him. He healed himself by praying in the following manner several times a day until he got the inner reaction which satisfied, "My associate, John, is loving, kind, and cooperative. He did not hurt, upset, or confuse me. I forgive myself completely for harboring revengeful, hateful thoughts about John. John is full of peace, joy, and love. There is harmony, peace, and understanding between us.

Whenever any negative thought about John or anyone else arises, I immediately remind myself that the peace of God flows through me."

How His Specific Prayer Worked

These spiritual thoughts released a tremendous, potent, therapeutic vibration which radiated throughout his mind and body, and all the cells of his body took on a new tone. Moreover, the spiritual vibrations destroyed the negative pattern lodged in the subconscious area of his mind, and he experienced a remarkable change for the better. In a few months' time he was discharged by his physician as cured and was free to eat his customary food.

Taking A Personal Inventory

Are you experiencing friction, misunderstanding, and resentment in your relationship with others? These unsatisfactory personal adjustments are due to the bad company you are keeping in your mind. When you were young, mother warned you to keep away from bad company, and if you disobeyed, you were probably soundly spanked. In a somewhat similar manner you must not walk down the dark alleys of your mind and keep the company of resentment, ill will, hostility, and hatred; these are the thieves of your mind which rob you of poise, balance, harmony, and health. You must positively and definitely refuse to walk and talk with them in the galleries of your mind. On the contrary you must make it a practice to walk the sunlit streets of your mind, associating with lovely, spiritual companions called confidence, peace, faith, love, joy, good will, health, happiness, guidance, inspiration, and abundance. You can choose your companions in the objective world, and I feel sure that when you do you will select them according to the criteria of honesty and integrity. You select your clothes, work, friends, teachers, books, home, and food. You are a choosing, volitional being. When you choose something, you portray a preference for one thing over another; it may be a hat or a pair of shoes. The Bible says, "Choose ye this day whom ye shall serve." Choose health and happiness in your mind.

Achieving Understanding

Man has to give up his false beliefs, opinions, and theories and exchange them for the truth which sets him free. He must learn that he is not a victim of his five senses; neither is he controlled by the external conditions or environment. He can change conditions by changing his mental attitude. His own thought and feeling create his destiny and determine his experience. Therefore, man no longer can blame others for his misery, pain, or failure. When a man sees clearly that which he thinks, feels, believes, and gives mental consent to, consciously or unconsciously, determines all happenings, events, and circumstances in his life, he ceases to resent, condemn, and blame others. He discovers there is no one to blame but himself.

Thoughts Are Things

For countless centuries man has looked outside of himself and has filled his mind with jealousies, hates, resentment, and depressions due to his belief that others were marring his happiness and causing his troubles. He has believed that he is the victim of fate, chance, accidents, and that there are other forces and powers inimical to his welfare. These beliefs, with others of a similar nature, are false for the simple reason that man's thoughts are things, and man is what he thinks all day long. His mind is full of all sorts of weird ideas, superstitions, fears, anxieties, and complicated philosophies about devils, evil entities, and malicious powers. Man's thought is creative; his thoughts become his ulcer or his poverty. Man must divest himself of all his erroneous and false concepts and realize that he makes his own hell and his own heaven here and now. A man can influence his subconscious positively or negatively. The subconscious mind is always amoral, impersonal, and has no ethics or sentiments. Hence, if man's thoughts are of an evil nature, the law of his subconscious mind will automatically bring these thoughts into form and experience. If man's thoughts are good, wholesome, and constructive, the law of his subconscious will bring forth good experiences and happy circumstances. This is neither more nor less than the law of cause and effect which is a universal and impersonal law.

We Punish Ourselves

The cause is thought, and the effect is the automatic reaction of the mind to the thought. Our retribution or reward depends on how we use our mind. If a man makes an erroneous decision in his mind, he invokes the mathematical and just response of the law and experiences loss as a result of his erroneous judgment or decision. The law of action and reaction is universal throughout nature. If man's thoughts are wise, his actions will be wise. God is not vengeful, but the impersonal laws of our own mind reacting according to their nature because of our thought-life produce what seems to look like vengeance to the man unawakened to the laws of his mind. Actually it is a natural law of action and reaction which is always equal, exact, and precise. There is no point in blaming the lake if a man should happen to fall in when he lacks the ability to swim. We would not accuse the lake of vengeance; the water was completely impersonal. Think good, good follows; think evil, and evil follows.

> "I sent my soul through the Invisible—
> Some letter of that after-Life to spell,
> And by and by my soul returned to me
> And answered, 'I myself am Heaven and Hell.'"
>
> OMAR KHAYYAM.

5

The Transforming Power of Prayer

It is important to recognize and use the power of prayer to transform all negative attitudes that precipitate the unfortunate circumstances in our daily activities and health. We are inclined to permit too many transient emotional reactions to upset the plans and hopes for the events of our lives, to disturb our relations with people, to cause us to rebel against the conditions of our environments. You will find many constructive changes in your relationship with the world when you come to know the power of prayer to sustain the warm kinship we should feel for friends and acquaintances, protecting us from the chilling changes of emotional uncertainties.

His Attitude Was All Wrong

A young engineer said to me some months ago, "The boss is an ignoramus, so I walked out. I just got another job, but I went from the frying pan into the fire. This place is worse." The young man had a domineering, tyrannical, puritanical sort of a father typical of his New England traditions. The youth had resented his father and had not written him for several years. Slowly but surely he began to see that he was rebelling against authority in the same way that he had been rebelling inwardly against his father. It began to dawn on him that he was actually transferring the blame for his own shortcomings, mistakes, and misdeeds to others and also was attributing to others his unacceptable impulses and thoughts.

His New Attitude

He decided to pray morning and evening as follows: "I wish for everyone in the plant where I work health, happiness, peace, and promotion. My employer congratulates me on my work; I paint this picture in my mind regularly and I know it will come to pass. I am loving, kind, and cooperative. I practice the Golden Rule and I sincerely treat everyone in the same way that I would like to be treated. Divine Intelligence rules and guides me all day long; I am prospered in all my ways." As he saturated his mind regularly and systematically with these spiritual thoughts, he succeeded in bringing about a new mental attitude of a constructive nature which changed everything for the better in his life.

Five Positions In Five Months

I gave advice to a young man one time who had lost five positions in five months. He drank excessively, was irresponsible, shiftless, lazy, indolent, crude, lacking in understanding, zeal, and application. I explained to him that his dominant attitude of mind colored everything, and that his gloomy outlook on life caused him to look at everything from the dark or negative side. The good news he received from his family from time to time brought about only an occasional mood of cheerfulness which was drowned out in a few minutes by his dominant, gloomy, depressed attitude.

Becoming A New Man

At my suggestion this young man took a course in public speaking and another course at night school where with diligence, personal initiative, and application he learned the rudiments of the commercial world. He began to pray for guidance and prosperity by claiming these qualities. Gradually he commenced to die to the "old man" and to put on the "new man." He developed enthusiasm, perseverance, stick-to-it-ive-ness, and became the foreman of the shop where he worked. He became happy and joyous and began to express health, harmony, and true living. He learned that practically all teaching, whether institutional, religious, or secular, has for its real purpose the inducement of a changed mental attitude towards life, people, and events. The first step in this young man's onward march was correcting his attitude towards life.

A Murderer Becomes A Teacher

I knew a murderer one time who confessed to me that he had killed a man. He had an intense desire to transform himself and be reborn mentally and spiritually. He had a very receptive attitude of mind and believed that "with God all things are possible." At my suggestion he started to still the wheels of his mind for fifteen or twenty minutes several times daily; then he would silently, quietly, and lovingly claim and feel that he was now a channel for God's love, peace, beauty, wisdom, and intelligence, and that his mind and heart were being cleansed, purified, healed, and restored. As he did this regularly, sincerely, and enthusiastically, he began to become more loving, more peaceful, and more kind in all his ways. An inner sense of peace welled up within him.

One night this man had an inner experience sometimes called conversion. He said that he seemed to be immersed in a blaze of Light. Actually he was blinded like Paul by the Light for a while. All he could remember was that he felt the ecstasy and rapture of God's Love. His feeling was indescribable. He was a changed man in his mind and heart and began to teach others how to live; he is still doing it.

Attitudes Conditioned By Imagination

Whatever you imagine a thing to be, there is a corresponding emotional reaction. A prominent eastern teacher of oriental philosophy while walking the streets of London in the twilight of the evening looked at a coiled rope on the street and imagined it to be a snake; he became paralyzed with fear. When he discovered his mistake, his true picture of the rope induced a new mental attitude and emotional response. What do you imagine yourself to be? What do you imagine Life to be? According to your imagination will it respond to you.

How She Got A New Attitude

A young lady had a music degree and wanted to teach music, but she had the attitude of mind that she would fail, that students would not come to her because she was unknown. She adopted a new attitude and began to realize and affirm boldly, "I can be what I want to be. I can do what I want to do through the Power of the Almighty within me." She came to the decision that a great number of students could be benefited by what she had to offer. Her basic trouble was fear and she overcame it through the frequent repetition of the above prayer and the disciplined use of her imagination. Twice daily she imagined herself teaching students and saw them happy and pleased. She was the actress in the drama. "Act as though I am, and I will be." She felt herself as the successful teacher, acted the role in her imagination, and focused her attention on her ideal. Through her persistence she became one with the idea in her mind until she succeeded in objectively expressing what she subjectively imagined and felt. What she imagined her life to be, she felt it to be, and according to her new feeling or mental attitude was it done unto her.

How A New Attitude Saved His Life

During a series of lectures in Capetown, South Africa, a brilliant lawyer listening to one of my lectures gave me a clipping dealing with forgiveness from a newspaper called Argus. I quote a few pertinent paragraphs. "Lieutenant Colonel J. P. Carne told of his life as a prisoner in Korea. During his eighteen months solitary confinement he did not have a bitter word for the action of his Chinese captors in imposing a sentence so harsh that doctors were amazed at his survival. When walking around his garden (in England) listening to the church bells welcoming him home, Lieutenant Colonel Carne said, 'The mental picture of this glorious place (his loved ones, his garden, his home) forever kept my mind alive. Not for one moment did I let it slip away.'" The caption of the article was *A Garden Gave Him Courage.*

This example is a beautiful lesson in the art of forgiving. Instead of resenting, hating, or indulging in mental recriminations, he gave himself a constructive vision. He imagined himself at home with his loved ones; he felt the thrill and joy of it all. Visualizing his garden in full bloom, he saw the plants grow and bring forth fruit. It was all vivid and real. He felt all this inwardly in his imagination. He said other men would have gone insane or perhaps have died of a broken heart, but he saved himself because he had a vision. "It was a vision I never let slip away." His great secret was a new mental attitude in the midst of privation, misery, and squalor. He was loyal to his mental picture and never deviated from it by destructive inner talking and negative mental imagery.

This Is The Last Straw

John was boiling and seething with resentment, saying to himself, "This I can't take after all my years of faithful service." He added that he had been smarting from a letter received from his general manager. His attitude was, "This is the last straw!" I explained to this young man that he was poisoning his whole system by his destructive mental attitude and that he had to reverse his mental picture. Here is a very old formula or technique which I gave him: Compose a letter, written as from the general manager to yourself, which would make you happy and satisfied if you received it. Put into this letter the words you would like the general manager to write or say to you. At night prior to sleep he imagined the general manager had written him a letter which praised him and his work and which made him happy and satisfied in every way according to the Golden Rule and the spirit of good will. He saw the words on the imaginary letter and rejoiced in reading them. As he said to me, "I kept it up every night. I would read that letter over and over again and look at the general manager's signature." All hatred left him as he continued to do this. To quote him again, "The queerest thing in all the world happened!" The general manager actually wrote him a letter praising and promoting him. The letter contained the essence of what he had been imagining and feeling for several days. Here is shown clearly what a new attitude of mind will do, substituting the mood of love and good will for the feeling of ill will and hostility. His new harmonious and cooperative attitude of mind was subconsciously felt by the general manager, causing him to respond in kind. He gave love and he received love. *Forgive (give for), and you shall be forgiven.* LUKE 6:37.

Why She Suffered For Years

I interviewed a young woman in Perth, Western Australia, some years ago, who suffered for years from migraine headaches, sinusitis, stomach trouble, and severe asthmatic attacks. She told me a sordid tale of bitterness, hostility, and hatred towards her mother. I asked her where her mother was, and she said, "Oh, she died ten years ago." It seems the mother left the estate to her sister in New Zealand. All this time she had been poisoning herself with that mental poison called hate. It is a real "killer."

Let Us Reason Together

In talking the matter over and reasoning it out, this young woman realized that her mother had acted according to her lights. Her mother had done what she felt was right according to her mental attitude. She learned that it was necessary to get a new mental attitude and pray for her mother, thereby blessing herself and her mother. She wept copiously, which was good. It was a release. She said, "God bless my mother, and His Love be with her wherever she is." This was the healing balm necessary; this was love and good will speaking. We prayed together for her mother, realizing that her mother was surrounded by love, peace, and beauty, that God's river of peace filled her soul, and that she was illumined and inspired by God. A wonderful change came over her. A light came into this woman's eyes, a smile appeared on her countenance, a radiance seemed to surround and envelop her. All hatred was melted in the sunshine of His Love.

Be ye transformed by the renewal of your mind.
Rom. 12:2.

6

How to Pray for Guidance

The power that moves the universe is the unlimited reservoir of the creative power within every individual. By learning to pray for guidance, man learns to tap these forces freely by simply decreeing the objectives for which he prays. However it is yet a mystery of the Infinite Mind as to *how, when, where, or through what source* the answers to prayer will come. The finite mind of man simply implants the thought in the subconscious mind through which agency the Infinite Mind works. Man in his prayers must learn not to limit the effectiveness of the reaction by attempting to make demands as to time, place, way.

Guidance Comes to Doctor
at End of His Rope

The subconscious mind guided Dr. A. J. Cronin, the well-known author of *The Cital, A Thing of Beauty,* and many other novels. He wrote an article in one of our local newspapers wherein he stated that after his health had broken down, he had to take a year's rest because he had been told that he might never again be fit to stand the wear and tear of medical life. At that time Dr. Cronin was on the threshold of achieving his highest ambition, that of becoming a specialist in Harley Street, London. A friend encouraged him with the thought, "You know, doctor, we have a saying in Ireland, if the good God shuts one door, He opens another."

Dr. Cronin wrote that some time afterward, while he was resting in the West Highlands, he was seized with an impulse to write. The result was *Hatter's Castle.* He sent the manuscript to a publisher and it was accepted. One door had been closed, but the wisdom of the subconscious mind had opened another to a very successful and lucrative career. It revealed to him special talents which he didn't know he possessed. Your subconscious mind will do the same for you when you trust it and believe that it has the answer.

Your Wishes Have A Way Of Coming True

The urge of everybody is to be, to do, and to have. Perhaps you are saying to yourself, "I wish to be an actor, actress, writer, engineer, or a great musician."

There was an article published in the *This Week* section of the *Los Angeles Times* a few years ago written by a leading musical star entitled "Watch Your Wishes."

In the article she says that wishes are thoughts vibrant with life and eager for action. They have the power to produce light and beauty. Everything she has wished for all her life has come to pass to the point where she "watches her wishes" to make sure they are of value.

. . . Just as a gardener cultivates his plot, keeping it free from weeds, and growing the flowers and fruits which he requires, so may a man tend the garden of his mind, weeding out all the wrong, useless, and impure thoughts, and cultivating toward perfection the flowers and fruits of right, useful, and pure thoughts. By pursuing this process, a man sooner or later discovers that he is the master-gardener of his soul, the director of his life . . . (Allen).

A Detective Gets His Man

Some months ago I told a prominent detective that he could solve his difficult case through the subconscious mind. I began my explanation in this way.

If, when you retire, you will tell your subconscious mind to awaken you at six a.m., it will do so. The reason is that you are thinking about six o'clock in the morning. Whenever you are definite in your conscious reasoning mind, you are automatically calling forth a response from the subconscious mind. When your thought is clear-cut and definite, and you believe in the power of the subconscious mind to answer, the response from your own subconscious mind will come quickly. I assured this detective that the subconscious mind knew where all the participants in the crime were, the whereabouts of their hideout, and the way to find them.

Everything that man has ever thought, a memory of everything that has ever transpired or occurred on this planet is recorded faithfully in the Universal Subconscious. And every man's personal subconscious is one with the Universal Subconscious, or as Carl Jung calls it, the collective unconscious of the race. I am using the word subconscious in this book in its broad sense, acknowledging that while we can use the subconscious mind two ways, negatively or positively, nevertheless lodged within the subconscious mind is the wisdom, power, intelligence, and love of the Infinite One or the God-Self.

Here is the simple technique I gave this outstanding detective: "Quiet your mind; still your body; tell your body to relax; it has to obey you. Your body has no volition, initiative, or intelligence of itself. It is an emotional disc which records your beliefs and impressions. Immobilize your attention; focus your thought on the solution to your problems. Try and solve them with your conscious mind. Think how happy you would be about the perfect solution. If your mind wanders bring it back gently. In this sleepy, drowsy state, say quietly and positively, 'The answer is mine now; I know my subconscious mind knows the answer.' Live now in the mood of the solution. Sense the feeling you would have if the perfect answer were yours now. Let your mind play with this mood in a relaxed way; then drop off to sleep. You may fall asleep sooner than you expected, but you were thinking about the answer; the time was not wasted. When you awaken and yet you do not have the answer, get busy about something else. Probably when you are preoccupied with your work, the answer will come into your mind like toast pops out of a toaster."

He followed these simple instructions, which may be used every night to solve any problems. On the morning of the fourth day following this procedure, the answer came into his conscious mind while he was shaving. The reason for this was that while he was shaving he was relaxed; then the wisdom and intuition of the subconscious mind came to his surface or conscious reasoning mind. The subconscious will give you guidance, but you must come to a definite conclusion or judgment in your conscious mind. *You must not vacillate or waver.* In other words you must make up your mind like the above-mentioned detective, and think and know that the answer or solution is yours because that which knows all and sees all is within you.

How To Stop Blocking The Answer

Men and women are constantly seeking solutions and answers to everyday problems such as the following: "Shall I accept this new position or stay where I am?" "Shall I invest in this property?" "Shall I keep or sell my home?" "Shall I dissolve partnership or enter into this new partnership?" "Shall I marry this person?" "I must get an answer before midnight, what decision shall I make?"

Many people unknowingly block the answers to these and other perplexing questions by failing to understand the workings of their deeper or subconscious mind. We must remember that whenever the subconscious *accepts* any idea, it immediately begins to execute it. It uses all its mighty resources to that end and mobilizes all the unlimited mental and spiritual powers in our depths. This law is true for good or bad ideas. Consequently, if we use it negatively, it brings trouble, failure, and confusion. When we use it positively, it brings guidance, freedom, and peace of mind. The right answer is inevitable when our thoughts are positive, constructive, and loving. From this it is perfectly obvious that the only thing we have to do is to get the subconscious to accept an idea by feeling its reality now, and the law of our mind will do the rest. We turn over the request with faith and confidence and the subconscious takes over.

We block our progress and answers to our problems by such statements as: "Things are getting worse." "I will never get the answer." "I see no way out." "It is hopeless." "I don't know what to do." "I'm all mixed up." When we use such statements, we get no response or cooperation from the subconscious mind. Like soldiers marking time, we neither go forward nor backward, in other words we don't get anywhere. If we should get into a taxi and give half a dozen different directions to the driver in five minutes, he would become hopelessly confused and probably would refuse to take us anywhere. It is the same when working with our subconscious mind. There must be a clear-cut idea in our minds. We must arrive at the definite decision that there is a way out, a solution to the vexing problems. The Infinite Intelligence within the subconscious knows only the answer. When we come to that clear-cut conclusion in our conscious minds, our minds are made up, and according to our belief is it done unto us.

Belief is simply a thought or concept held in the mind, and whatever the nature of that thought, a corresponding response shall come forth. If our concept is "There is no way out," or "I can't get an answer," we will call forth a definite response of confusion and chaos. If our thought is wise, the reaction or response will be wise. We all know that an action is only the outer expression of a thought. Our constructive action or decision is but the manifestation of a wise or true thought entertained in our mind. Common sense is an expression of inner guidance or wisdom. After asking for guidance or an answer, we do not neglect obvious and convenient stepping stones to our goal. We avoid blocking our answer when we simply think about the solution, knowing that our thought activates the subconscious which knows all, sees all, and has the "know how" of accomplishment.

You Can Choose Confidence, Triumph, and Victory

The Bible says, *Choose ye this day whom ye shall serve.* The key to health, happiness, peace of mind, and abundance lies in the capacity to choose. When we learn to think right, we will stop choosing pain, misery, poverty, and limitation. On the contrary we will choose from the treasure house of Infinity within us. Each one will say incisively and decisively, "I choose happiness, peace, prosperity, wisdom, and security." The moment we come to that definite conclusion in our conscious mind, our subconscious mind, backed by the Power and Wisdom of the Infinite, will come to our aid. Guidance will come, and the way or path of achievement will be revealed to us. Claim definitely and positively without the slightest hesitation, doubt, or fear, "There is only one power of creation and it is the power of my own deeper self. There is a solution to every problem. This I know, decree, and believe." As we affirm these truths boldly, we will receive guidance, and the steps we should take will be revealed to us.

Lost In the Jungle, and How to Get Out

In using the subconscious mind we must remember it reasons deductively. It sees the end only, thereby bringing to a logical, sequential conclusion the nature of the premise in the conscious mind.

When I was about eleven years old, I was lost in the jungle. At first I was terrified and then I began to claim that God would lead me out. I was seized with an overpowering hunch to travel in a certain direction. This inner push or tendency of the subconscious, which I followed, proved to be correct and I was miraculously led into the arms of a searching party after two days time. This lead was the prompting of the subconscious mind which knew the way out of the jungle.

Many people live in a mental jungle of confused, fearful, and neurotic thoughts. The way out of this jungle is very clear. Claim very strongly that the subconscious wisdom within is bringing order, peace, and harmony into your life. As you do this regularly and systematically, right results follow inevitably because the wisdom, power, and love of the infinite resources of the subconscious are moving on your behalf. The omnipotent powers of the subconscious cannot fail.

Plant Orchids In The Garden of Mind

Think of a garden, then you will understand the two-fold aspect of mind and subjective law by which it operates. The conscious mind plants the seeds in the soil. It decides what kind of seeds shall be planted. As you know, the soil will grow whatever is planted in it, be it grapes or thorns.

Similarly, look upon the subconscious mind as the soil. It contains all of the elements essential for growth. Again let us realize it is the nature of the soil to bring forth, but as you know it is not concerned in the slightest with what it brings forth. It does not care whether it brings forth poison ivy or an orchid. All of the laws of nature would be violated should the soil refuse to produce or grow poisonous plants, if this is what the conscious mind elected to grow.

Exactly the same thing is true of the subconscious mind. It is a doer; it never questions or talks back. It accepts what is deposited and produces it in your experience whether it is good or bad. Plant *whatsoever things are true, just, pure, lovely, noble, and of good report*, and orchids will blossom in the garden of your mind, body, and experience.

The Secret of Right Action

Devote yourself mentally to the right answer until you find its response in you. The response is a feeling, an inner awareness, an overpowering hunch whereby you know that you know. You have used the power and wisdom of the subconscious to the point where it begins to use you.

I was praying for a boy in the last World War. His mother told me that she had received a telegram stating he had been killed in action. I felt that this was untrue and told her so. I couldn't prove it objectively, but subjectively I had an overpowering conviction that he was alive. Subsequent events verified this conviction. There had been an error. He was and is very much alive.

You cannot possibly fail or make one false step while believing in and operating under the direction of the subconscious wisdom within you. You receive guidance in accordance with your habitual thinking. If you think and dwell upon fears, troubles, and failures, you will be guided in the wrong direction, and more chaos and confusion will be experienced.

Take this great thought and dwell upon it. There is nothing to fear in all of the universe! You have the power and control through the wise use of your subconscious mind. Make up your mind once and for all that within you is the answer to all problems. This conviction activates the subconscious power and sets its wisdom and beneficence into operation for you.

Sit down quietly now and imagine a beautiful lake in the mountains. On the surface of the quiet lake you see mirrored the stars, moon, and the nearby trees. If the lake is disturbed you will not see the reflection. *Similarly, quiet your mind, relax, and let go.* Think of peace and stillness. *Know the true answer always comes in peace.* Then over the mirrored waters of your mind will move the answer to your question.

7

How Prayer Removes
the Road Blocks

Mr. Block said that he had been making an annual income of $20,000, but for the past three months all doors seemed to jam tightly. He brought clients up to the point where they were about to sign on the dotted line, and at the eleventh hour the door closed. He added that perhaps a jinx was following him.

In discussing the matter with Mr. Block, I discovered that three months previously he had become very irritated, annoyed, and resentful toward a dentist who, after he had promised to sign a contract, had withdrawn at the last moment. He began to live in the unconscious fear that other clients would do the same, thereby setting up a history of frustration, hostility, and obstacles. He gradually built up in his mind a belief in obstructions and last minute cancellations until a vicious circle had been established. "What I fear most has come upon me." Mr. Block realized that the trouble was in his own mind, and that it was essential to change his mental attitude.

His run of so-called misfortune was broken in the following way: "I realize I am one with the Infinite which knows no obstacle, difficulty, or delay. I live in the joyous expectancy of the best. The deeper mind responds to my thoughts. I know that the work of the Infinite cannot be hindered. God always finishes successfully whatever He begins. God works through me bringing all my plans and purposes to completion. Whatever I start, I bring to a successful conclusion. My aim is to give wonderful service, and all those whom I contact are blessed by what I have to offer. All my work renders full fruition. I thank God for this."

He repeated this prayer every morning before going to call on his customers and he prayed also each night prior to sleep. In a short time he was back in his old, accustomed stride as a successful salesman.

Cause and Effect

Mr. Block removed the mental road blocks after he realized that whatever he experienced in his life was really the outpicturing of his own thought and belief.

When he changed his thought, the outer picture changed also. He found that the story of his life was really the story of the relations between himself and God.

The Alcoholic's Road Block

Mr. Barleycorn visited me one day when I was giving some lectures in Auckland, New Zealand. A chronic alcoholic, he had tried all the "cures" to no avail, asserting that an uncontrollable passion seized him periodically to drink. He was a victim of a habit, and because the acts leading to intoxication were repeated so often, he had established a subjective pattern in his subconscious mind.

Because the alcoholic has yielded so many times to his craving, he fears that he will yield once more; this contributes to his repeated falls due to the suggestions given to his subconscious mind. It is his imagination which causes the alcoholic to return to drinking inter-mittently. The images which have been impressed on his subconscious mind begin to bear fruit. He imag-ines a drinking bout in which glasses are filled and drained; then he imagines the following sense of ease and en- joyment, a feeling of relaxation. If he lets his imagination run wild, he will go to the bar or buy a bottle.

The drinker uses effort and will power to over-come the habit, or "cause," as he is likely to call it. But the more effort or will power he uses, the more hope-lessly does he become engulfed in the quicksand of good intentions.

Law Of Reversed Effort

Effort is invariably self-defeated, eventuating always in the opposite of what is desired. The reason for this is obvious. The suggestions of powerlessness to over-come the habit dominate his mind; the subconscious mind is always controlled by the dominant idea. The subconscious mind will accept the strongest of two contradictory propositions. The effortless way is the best.

In 1910 the French School of Therapeutics explained what they termed the law of reversed effort. When your desire and your imagination are in con-flict, the imagination invariably gains the day. For example, you will hear an alcoholic say, "I took a lot of pains, I tried so hard, I forced myself, I used all the will power I had." He has to be made to realize that his error lies in the effort; then he begins to conquer the habit.

If, for example, you were asked to walk a plank on the floor, you would do so without question. Now suppose the same plank were placed twenty feet up in the air between two walls, would you walk it? Your desire to walk it would be counteracted by your imagination—your mental road block would be your fear of falling. The dominant idea would conquer. Your desire, will, or effort to walk would be reversed, and the dominant idea of failure would be reinforced.

If a man says, "I want to give up alcohol, but I cannot," he may wish to give it up, but the harder he tries the less he is able to do so. Never try to compel the subconscious mind to accept your idea by exercising will power. Such attempts are doomed to failure. The subconscious mind accepts the dominant of two contradictory statements. It is like the man who is poverty-stricken saying, "I am wealthy." In most instances his statement makes him poorer. The simple reason for this is that his belief in poverty is so much greater than his belief in abundance that he is suggesting more lack to himself each time he makes the statement. This illustrates the law of reversed effort. In other words his subconscious mind reacts with the opposite result from that which was intended.

Cause For Repeated Failures

I told Mr. Barleycorn about an alcoholic in Rochester, New York, whom I had treated some years earlier.

That man said to me, "I would not drink a drop of liquor for six months and I would congratulate myself. All my friends would pat me on the back telling me what wonderful will power I had."

"Then," he added, "an uncontrollable urge would seize me, and I would be drunk for two weeks." This had happened time and again with this man. The efforts of his will would suppress his desire temporarily, but his continued efforts to suppress the many urges made matters worse. His repeated failures convinced him that he was hopeless and powerless to control his urge or obsession. This idea of being powerless operated, of course, as a powerful suggestion to his subconscious mind, increased his impotence, and made his life a succession of failures.

I taught him to *harmonize the functions of the conscious and subconscious mind. When these two cooperate, the idea or desire implanted in the subconscious mind is realized.* His reasoning mind admitted that if he had been conditioned negatively, he could be conditioned positively. His mind entertained the idea that he could succeed. He ceased thinking of the fact that he was powerless to overcome the habit. Moreover, he understood clearly that there was no obstacle to his healing other than his own thought; therefore, there was no occasion for great mental effort or mental coercion. To use force is to pre-suppose that there is opposition. When the mind is concentrated on the means to overcome a problem, it is no longer concerned with the obstacle.

The Power of His Mental Picture

This man made a practice of relaxing his body, getting into a relaxed, drowsy, meditative state; then he filled his mind with the picture of the desired end, knowing that the subconscious mind would bring it about in the easiest way. He imagined his daughter congratulating him on his freedom, saying to him, "Daddy, it's wonderful to have you home!" He had lost his family through drink. He was not allowed to visit them; his wife would not speak to him.

Regularly, systematically, he used to sit down and meditate in the way outlined. When his attention wandered, he brought it back to the picture of his daughter with her smile, and the scene of his own home enlivened by her cheery tonal qualities. All this brought about a reconditioning of his mind. It was a gradual process. He kept it up; he persevered knowing that sooner or later he would succeed in impregnating his subconscious mind with the mental picture. I had told him that the conscious mind was the camera, and his subconscious mind was the sensitive plate on which he registered and impressed the picture. This had made a profound impression on him; his whole aim was to impress the picture and develop it in his mind. Films are developed in the dark; likewise, mental pictures are developed in the darkroom of the subconscious mind.

Focused Attention

Realizing that his conscious mind was simply a camera, he used no effort. There was no mental struggle. He quietly adjusted his thought and focused his attention on the scene before him until he gradually became identified with the picture. He became absorbed in the mental atmosphere, repeating the mental movie frequently. There was no room for doubt that a healing would follow. When there was any temptation to drink, he would switch his imagination from any reveries of drinking bouts to the feeling of being at home with the family. He was successful because he confidently expected to experience the picture he was developing in his mind. Today he is the president of a multimillion dollar concern and is radiantly happy.

Cause of Alcoholism

The real cause of alcoholism is negative and destructive thinking; for as a man thinketh so is he. The alcoholic has a deep sense of inferiority, inadequacy, defeat, and frustration, usually accompanied by a deep inner hostility. He has countless alibis as to his reasons for drinking, but the sole reason is in his *thought life*. If you are an alcoholic, admit it; do not dodge the issue. Many people remain alcoholics because they refuse to admit it.

Your disease is an instability, an inner fear. You are refusing to face life and so you try to escape your responsibilities through the bottle. The interesting thing about an alcoholic is that he has no free will; he thinks he has; he boasts about his will power. The habitual drunkard says bravely, "I will not touch it any more," but he has no power to back up his statement.

There are many people who find themselves in the same condition as Mr. Barleycorn. As soon as they are made to realize that the problem of alcoholism is of their own making and that they are living in their own psychological prison of fear, false beliefs, resentment, hostility, they are ready to recondition themselves to react in a constructive way. The minute they express a keen desire to free themselves from previous habits, they are fifty-one per cent healed. Now they can follow a program of prayer to remove the mental blocks.

Technique of Healing Used

There is nothing new about the following technique which Mr. Barleycorn used. It is as old as man. The most ancient wisdom available said, "As a man imagines and feels, so is he."

The first step: Get still; quiet the wheels of the mind. Enter into a sleepy, drowsy state. In this relaxed, peaceful, receptive state you are preparing for the second step.

The second step: Take a brief phrase which can readily be graven on the memory and repeat it over and over again as a lullaby. (Nancy School Technique). Use the phrase, "Sobriety and peace of mind are mine now, and I give thanks." To prevent the mind from wandering, repeat it aloud or sketch its pronunciation with the lips and tongue as you say it mentally. This helps its entry into the subconscious mind. Do this for five minutes or more. You will find a deep emotional response from the subconscious mind.

The third step: Just before going to sleep, practice what Goethe used to do: Imagine a friend, a loved one in front of you. Your eyes are closed; you are relaxed and at peace. The loved one is subjectively present and is saying to you, "Congratulations!" You see the smile; you hear the voice. You touch the hand and the face; it is all so real and vivid. The word *congratula-*

tions implies complete freedom. Hear it over and over again until you get the reaction which satisfies.

Use the above technique three or four times a day and at night prior to sleep. Imagine the end—victory. See fulfillment and accomplishment and maintain this faith every step of the way, knowing that having imagined and felt the end, you have willed the means to the realization of the end.

I am now thinking of a married man with four children, supporting and secretly living with another woman during his business trips. He was ill, nervous, irritable, cantankerous, and could not sleep without drugs. He had pains in numerous organs of his body which doctors could not diagnose. He was a confirmed alcoholic when I saw him. The reason for his periodic sprees was a deep, unconscious sense of guilt. He had violated the ancient code and this troubled him. The religious creed he was brought up on was deeply lodged in his subconscious mind; he drank excessively to heal the wound of guilt. Some invalids take morphine and codeine for severe pains; he was taking alcohol for the pain or wound in his mind. It was the old story of adding fuel to the fire.

He listened to the explanation of how his mind worked, he faced his problem, looked at it, and gave up his dual role. He knew that his drinking was an unconscious attempt to escape. The hidden cause lodged in the subconscious mind had to be eradicated; then the healing followed.

When he began to look at his problem in the light of reason, it was dissipated. He began to use this treatment three or four times a day. "My mind is full of peace, poise, balance, and equilibrium. The Infinite Power lies stretched in smiling repose within me. I am not afraid of anything in the past, the present, or the future. Infinite Intelligence leads, guides, and directs me in all ways. I now meet every situation with faith, poise, calmness, and confidence. I am now completely free from the habit; my mind is full of inner peace, freedom, and joy. I forgive myself; then I am forgiven. Peace, sobriety, and confidence reign supreme in my mind."

He repeated this frequently, knowing what he was doing and why he was doing it. Knowing what he was doing gave him the necessary faith and confidence. I explained to him that as he spoke these statements out loud, slowly, lovingly, and meaningfully, they would gradually sink down into his subconscious mind; like seeds, they would grow after their kind. I explained to him that his subconscious mind was like a garden; by planting lovely seeds he would reap a wonderful harvest. It is the nature of an apple seed to bring forth an apple tree. These truths on which he concentrated went in through his eyes, his ears heard the sound, the healing vibrations of these words reached his subconscious mind and obliterated all the negative mental patterns which caused all the trouble. Light dispels darkness; the positive thought destroys the negative. He became a transformed man within a month.

Keep On Keeping On

When fear knocks at your door or when worry, anxiety, and doubt cross your mind, behold your vision. Think of God, believe in Him, and an Almighty Power will be generated by your subconscious mind, giving you full confidence and strength. Keep on keeping on "Until the day breaks and the shadows flee away."

8

How to Forgive Through Prayer

Essentially we must make our peace with our fellowmen before we can pray effectively. But I have found that some definite formulas of prayer help people to resolve the frictions and misunderstandings that occur daily in the home and at business. A constructive restatement of the problem can hasten the reestablishment of harmony between all parties concerned.

A man recently came to my office in a very angry mood. A fellow-employee had been circulating a rumor that he had been falsifying some records. He denied emphatically that there was any truth to the report.

I assured him that what his fellow-employee was saying amounted to a lie, and that a lie cannot stand in the presence of the truth. I advised him to become calm and quietly claim that there existed perfect harmony, peace, and understanding between him and his associate.

He was quick to see the point. He affirmed that his associate knew the truth, spoke the truth, and that understanding reigned supreme between them. When, in due course, there developed a very happy relationship between the two men, the first man found that the trouble had originated in his own ridicule of a suggestion the other had made at an earlier conference. When he understood this, my friend decided to temper any criticism with tact and diplomacy; he had suffered from the backfire of ridicule. Freed from the feelings of anger and resentment, he enjoyed the moods of understanding and good will.

Learning to be Grateful for Criticism

I was talking to a teacher the other day. Someone had written her a critical letter saying she spoke too fast, she swallowed some of her words, she couldn't be heard, her diction was poor, and her speech ineffective. This teacher was furious but she had to admit that the criticisms were just. Her first reaction was childish; then she agreed that the letter was really a blessing and a marvelous corrective, so she proceeded immediately to supplement the deficiencies in her speech by enrolling for a course in public speaking at

City College. She wrote and thanked the writer of the note for her interest, expressing appreciation for her conclusions and findings which enabled the teacher to correct the matter at once.

How to be Compassionate

Suppose none of the things mentioned in the letter had been true of the speaker, the latter would have realized that her class material had upset the prejudices, superstitions, or narrow sectarian beliefs of the writer of the note, and that a psychologically ill person was simply pouring forth her resentment because a psychological boil had been hurt. To understand the fact is to become compassionate; the next logical step would be to pray for the other person's peace, harmony, and understanding. No criticism can affect you without your mental consent. You always should be master of your thoughts, reactions, and emotions. Emotion follows thought, and you have the power to reject all thoughts which may disturb or upset you.

Stop Blaming God

A man said to me one time that he would be all right if God would only leave him alone. He thought God was punishing him and putting obstacles in his way, and that this was the reason for his sickness and business failure. I asked him, "What is God?" He replied, "The Bible says 'God is love.'" A God of love is the answer to all our problems.

What Is God And Where Is God

Jesus called God "Our Father," which means that he taught that all of us have a common Father, that we are all brothers and sisters. God is Life; all of us and all things come forth from the One Life Principle. The word *father* denotes love, care, protection, provider. The word *father* means also the Creator, the Creative Principle of Life, the Infinite Power, the Supreme Being from which all things flow. Jesus said that "God is Spirit." You cannot see spirit; it is formless and shapeless. You do not see your mind, your spirit, which is God in you. God is inside and outside of everyone for God or Life is Omnipresent. God is in our own mind or consciousness. Locate God within you. When you say, "Heaven," it means the Invisible Spiritual Power without face, form, or figure. "It is the Father within which doeth the works." For instance, when you push a chair aside, it is not your body doing it, it is the Spirit within, the Creative Power, or God. When you walk, or lift the receiver, it is the Invisible Presence in you acting in the body, telephone, or typewriter, as the case may be. The Unmoved Mover of all is within you. Our Father is the name given to this God-Power or Presence within us to remind us It is a Beneficent, Kindly Power. The finite mind can never fully comprehend the Infinite, but one can certainly learn about the inner powers. We can learn the power of our thoughts and feelings, our actions and reactions, and there is much we can learn about the laws of our own being.

Healing Through Forgiveness

I spoke to the above-mentioned business man as follows: "If you think of God as cruel, tyrannical, and vengeful, you experience the results of your negative thinking. If you think God is punishing you or testing you, your own negative thought and imagery impressed in your subconscious mind cause you to suffer accordingly. You are actually punishing yourself."

When he saw the point, he made it a habit to pray several times a day as follows: "I know God is a Loving Father, the Life of me, who watches over me, cares for me, guides me, and inspires me. This Spiritual Power responds as a blessing and benediction to me. God is prospering me in all my ways, and I am divinely expressed. I know the Kingdom of Heaven is within me which means Infinite Intelligence, Boundless Wisdom, Absolute Harmony, Infinite Love, Omnipotence, and all the qualities and attributes of God are in my subconscious depths. I am now reproducing all the qualities and potencies of God by thinking of God and His Love, and I am moving onward, upward, and Godward."

He prayed along these lines several times a day. By enthroning this new concept of God in his mind and living with it, his whole world magically melted into the image and likeness of his habitual concept. By mentally dwelling on this concept of God, he experienced the reaction as love, peace, inspiration, and energy. He now looked upon God as a Father who loved, cared, and sent good things into his life. His business began to prosper, the organs of his body were restored to normal functioning, and he is now experiencing the joy of living. He *forgave* himself; he gave himself a new concept of God for the old idea of an inscrutable, tyrannical, despotic monarch living in the skies somewhere.

Cease Being Double Minded

No man can serve two masters. A man cannot expect to realize the desire of his heart if he believes there is a power which thwarts that desire. This creates a conflict and his mind is divided. He stands still and gets nowhere. His mind must move as a unity. Infinity cannot be divided or multiplied. The Infinite must be one—a unity; there cannot be two Infinites, as one would quarrel with the other; they would neutralize or cancel out each other. We would have a chaos instead of a cosmos. Unity of the spirit is a mathematical necessity, and there is no opposition to the One Power. If there were some power to challenge God or the Infinite One, God would cease to be Omnipotent or Supreme.

You can now see what confusion and chaos reign in the minds of people who believe in two opposing powers. Their minds are divided because they have two masters; this belief creates a conflict, causing their power and strength to be divided. Learn to go in one direction only by believing that the God who gave you the desire will also show you how to fulfill it. The Bible speaks emphatically about the One Power when it says, "Hear, O Israel: the Lord our God is one Lord."

How Much Do You Want What You Want?

A young man asked Socrates how he could get wisdom. Socrates replied, "Come with me."

He took the lad to a river, pushed the boy's head under the water, held it there until the boy was gasping for air, then relaxed and released his head. When the boy regained his composure, he asked him, "What did you desire most when you were under water?"

"I wanted air," said the boy.

Socrates said to him, "When you want wisdom as much as you wanted air when you were immersed in the water, you will receive it."

The man who *really* wants peace of mind and inner calm will get it. Regardless of how unjustly he has been treated, or how unfair the boss has been, or what a mean scoundrel someone proved to be, all this makes no difference to the spiritually-minded man. He knows what he wants, and he refuses to let the thieves of hatred, anger, hostility, and ill will rob him of peace, harmony, health, and happiness. He knows the ideal way. He ceases to become upset by people, conditions, news, events, by identifying his thoughts immediately with his aim in life. His aim is peace, health, inspiration, guidance, love, good will, harmony, and abundance. It is not difficult to mentally identify with peace and silently affirm that "God's river of peace flows through me now." Man's thought is the immaterial or invisible power, and he chooses to let it bless, inspire, and give him peace.

She Got Another Boyfriend

I was interested and amused in observing the reaction of Robert, a student of physics, to a telephone call from his girl friend. She informed him that she had another boy friend, and would not see him any more. He wished her happiness and good luck; then he said to me, "Shall I waste my energy by getting irritated and upset over this girl, or shall I apply my energy to the study of physics for the examination tomorrow?" He chose the latter idea.

This is an excellent way to forgive (give for) yourself. You can become calm, cool, and objective like that. It makes good sense. (Incidentally, I might add that Robert attracted another very beautiful girl the next day).

Left At The Altar

Some years ago I visited a church to perform a marriage ceremony. The young man did not appear, and at the end of two hours the bride-to-be shed a few tears; then she said to me, "I prayed for God's guidance; this is indeed His answer for He never faileth." That was her reaction—faith in God which healed her instantaneously. Someone else having a similar experience would have gone into a tantrum, have had emotional fits, required sedation and perhaps hospitalization.

Tune in with the Infinite and His Love, trusting the God-Power in the same way that you trusted your mother when she held you in her arms. This is how you can acquire poise and mental and emotional health.

People Don't Treat Me Right

Man must look in the right place to find the cause of his troubles; that place is within himself. The conversation of an emotionally immature person usually runs to explanatory excuses. "Others are antagonistic toward me." "People don't treat me right." "People are mean and unkind."

The sign of an adult, or an emotionally mature person, is that he does the best he can where he is. He knows that when others are cantankerous, irritable, crotchety, and cynical they are psychologically ill. He has compassion, understanding, and adjusts himself to people. He knows that many people are mentally ill and that he has no right to condemn ill people; therefore he blesses them and reacts positively and affirmatively.

We must really take an honest look at ourselves when we say that others annoy, upset, and don't treat us right. A good thing to do would be to see if we have been thinking of or expecting difficulties, delays, obstructions, and impediments. Perhaps we have been picturing resistance and opposition to our plans and purposes. If we are indulging in this type of mental imagery and patterns, we must expect the projection of such states into our business and social world. The result of this will be the unpleasant reactions of others. We learn to forgive when we learn there is really no one to blame but ourselves.

San Francisco Versus Los Angeles

A sales manager here in Los Angeles told me about one of his men in San Francisco who wrote and said that the people up there were very difficult to sell; he added that the price of the product was too high and that he wanted a transfer. The sales manager gave him a transfer to Los Angeles and sent another salesman to the same district in San Francisco. The second man got immediate results and wrote saying that the product was selling very well. The man who was transferred back to Los Angeles was amazed when he was confronted with the successful reports of the other salesman.

All this illustrates that our disturbed, hostile, resentful attitudes are reflected in our business, social life, financial life, as well as in our body and environment. The sales manager told me that envy and jealousy were the reasons for the poor showing of the first salesman. He was deeply resentful of the promotion of other men over whom he claimed seniority. He pointed out the length of his service; he criticized the management, arguing that you had to know the right people in order to get ahead. Yet all the time his inner upset condition was the cause of the decline in his sales.

To Understand All Is To Forgive All

When man understands the creative law of his own mind, he ceases to blame other people and conditions for making or marring his life. He knows that his own thought and feeling create his destiny; furthermore, he is aware that externals are not the causes and conditioners of his life and his experiences. To think that others can mar his happiness, that he is the football of a cruel fate, that he must oppose and fight others for a living—all these and others like them are untenable when he understands that *thoughts are things.* The Bible says the same thing. *For as he thinketh in his heart, so is he.* Prov. 23:7.

9

How Prayer Solves Marital Problems

Friction between husband and wife can be solved through prayer. By praying together they start together. Love unites and hate divides. The contemplation of divine ideals, the study of the laws of life, a common plan and purpose, and personal freedom bring about that harmonious marriage, the wedded bliss, that holy union where the two become one. Each is mentally and emotionally united with God. God is Love. To be real, marriage must first be spiritual, marriage must be of the heart. The *heart* is the chalice of God's presence. If both hearts are moved by love, sincerity, and honesty, God's love unites husband and wife; truly theirs is the marriage made in heaven.

How To Pray For Right Mate

The best time to prevent divorce is before marriage. A man or woman desiring to marry should pray to attract the right mate. The following prayers will prove very effective.

How To Attract The Ideal Husband

I know that I am one with God now. In Him I live, move, and have by being. God is Life; this life is the life of all men and women. We are all sons and daughters of the one Father.

I know and believe there is a man waiting to love and cherish me. I know I can contribute to his happiness and peace. He loves my ideals, and I love his ideals. He does not want to make me over; neither do I want to make him over. There is mutual love, freedom, and respect.

There is one mind; I know him now in this mind. I unite now with the qualities and attributes that I admire and want expressed by my husband. I am one with them in my mind. We know and love each other already in Divine Mind. I see the God in him; he sees the God in me. Having met him *within*, I must meet him in the *without*; for this is the law of my own mind.

These words go forth and accomplish whereunto they are sent. I know it is now done, finished, and accomplished in God. Thank you, Father.

How To Attract The Ideal Wife

God is One and Indivisible. In Him we love, move, and have our being. I know and believe that God indwells every person; I am one with God and with all people. I now attract the right woman who is in complete accord with me. This is a spiritual union, because it is the spirit of God functioning through the personality of someone with whom I blend perfectly. I know I can give to this woman love, light, and truth. I know I can make this woman's life full, complete, and wonderful.

I now decree that she possesses the following qualities and attributes; i.e., she is spiritual, loyal, faithful, and true. She is harmonious, peaceful, and happy. We are irresistibly attracted to each other. Only that which belongs to love, truth, and wholeness can enter my experience. I accept my ideal companion now.

As you think quietly and with interest on the qualities and attributes which you admire in the companion you seek, you will build the mental equivalent into your mentality; then the deeper currents of your subconscious mind will bring both of you together in divine order.

Steps In Prayer To Preserve Marriage

The first step: Never carry over from one day to another accumulated irritations arising from little disappointments. Be sure to forgive each other for any sharpness before you retire at night. The moment you awaken in the morning, claim Divine Intelligence is guiding you in all ways. Send out loving thoughts of peace, harmony, and love to your marriage partner, to all members of the family, and to the whole world.

The second step: Say grace at breakfast. Give thanks for the wonderful food, for your abundance, and for *all* of your blessings. Make sure that no problems, worries, or arguments shall enter into the table conversation; the same applies at dinner time. Say to your wife or husband, "I appreciate all you are doing, and I radiate love and good will to you all day long."

The third step: Husband and wife should alternate in praying each night. Do not take your marriage partner for granted; show your appreciation and your love. Think appreciation and good will, rather than condemnation, criticism, and nagging. The way to build a peaceful home and a happy marriage is upon the basis of love, beauty, harmony, mutual respect, faith in God, and in all things good. Read the 23rd,

91st, and 27th Psalms, the 11th Chapter, Hebrews, the 13th Chapter, I Corinthians, and other great texts of the New Testament before going to sleep. Say quietly, "Thank you, Father, for all the blessings of the day. God giveth his beloved sleep."

The above prayer therapy and belief in a Divine Intelligence develops strength, power, and love in the marriage relationship, as well as in all other phases of life. Husbands and wives will find themselves refreshed, rejuvenated, and invigorated by charging their batteries regularly and systematically with spiritual medicine.

I spoke to a woman some time ago who told me that her husband showered gifts upon her and brought toys home almost every night to their two children; yet he was irritable, ill-tempered, cursed the children, and snapped at her about the least thing. In talking to the man, I discovered that he wanted to be "free," as he called it, and wanted to avoid the responsibilities of marriage and fatherhood. Furthermore, he had a deep-seated guilt complex because he was having an affair with another woman and paying all the expenses for her apartment and clothes. The gifts which he brought to his family every night were his way of compensating for his guilty feelings and inner hostility which he felt toward them.

Fear Of Punishment

This man had high blood pressure and ulcers of the stomach which undoubtedly were due to his feelings of guilt and self-condemnation over forbidden behavior. He had a hidden fear of punishment for his actions. His obsessive thought resulted in considerable self-demotion, and his gifts to his wife and children were his way of expiation and atonement.

Turning Discord Into Harmony

This man was open and receptive to the explanation which I offered and he began to realize that he had some mental work that had to be done immediately. He had to give up his resentment, hostility, and ill will, and build a more harmonious and peaceful existence. He cut off relations with the other woman and began to pray along these lines several times a day: "Infinite Intelligence rules and guides me and I radiate love, peace, joy and good will to my wife and children. I surround my wife and children with the circle of God's love, knowing and believing that His love, peace, harmony, and joy fill their minds and hearts. I forgive myself and I feel free. I mean this, I am sincere, and I know the peace of God reigns supreme in my home, in my heart, and in my family."

By practicing this simple phase of the laws of mind, he replaced his inner turmoil with peace and good will. His new attitude dissolved his bodily ailment and brought peace to his troubled mind. He and his wife prayed together every night. Love was now ruling his home-life, and love dissolves everything unlike itself, for God is Love.

The Ouija Board and the Explanation

A husband said to me that he was being sued for divorce because the Ouija board told his wife he was unfaithful. At my request she came to see me. I explained to her in detail that it was her own subconscious mind which was confirming her suspicion and resentment toward her husband. She began to see clearly that it was her deeper mind which, through imperceptible movement of her fingers, operated the Ouija board. In other words, she was simply talking to herself. In talking to her husband I found out that he was impotent and was taking a series of hormone injections from a physician. This woman was honest enough with herself to see her error and both of them agreed to send thoughts of love, peace, and kindliness to one another. This dissolved the negative attitude and brought peace where discord and suspicion reigned. The explanation was the cure.

Emotional Blackmail Versus
A New Honeymoon

A woman was about to break up her home because, as she said, her husband no longer loved her. She wanted a home, but he preferred to live in an apartment. They couldn't agree. She told him that he didn't love her or care for her because he would not get the home. Also, she told me that she knew he didn't care any more because he smoked constantly, even though he knew that she was allergic to cigarette smoke.

She Wanted To Change Him

It takes two to make a quarrel. In this instance the woman was certainly emotionally immature. The reason she nagged him was that she wished to change his habits and make him feel guilty for going against her deep desires and wishes. I asked to see her husband and I found he was deeply resentful. He had a guilt-complex and responded to his wife by cutting, critical, and angry remarks over trivial and inconsequential things. It never pays to try and coerce another into going your way by subtly trying to make him or her feel guilty and hurt by not pleasing you.

The Price of Resentment

Resentment is one of the most expensive things in the world. It robs man of peace, health, vitality, and a sound mind, leaving him a mental and physical wreck. If continued or indulged in over a long period of time, the person becomes, cold, hard, callous, ossified, petrified, and he begins to resent everyone.

Saving the Marriage

In my presence the husband and wife talked over their difficulties, resentments, and hostilities, and learned to look at the facts. Each one looked at the situation objectively and they agreed that they had been childish. They also realized that by calmly talking out their difficulties in the spirit of love and harmony, agreement could be reached along all lines.

The Wife's Asthma

She discovered that her asthma was not caused by cigarette smoke, but by a deep hatred embodied in her subconscious mind. In psychosomatic circles there is a term, *organ specificity*, which means that resentment or hatred will cause asthma in one individual, high blood pressure in another, arthritis in a third, and perhaps migraine in still another. The fact is that any mental and emotional disturbance may influence practically any physiological process, and the symptoms and organs of the body affected depend on the sensitivity and constitutional make-up of the individual.

The Happy Ending

The wife's asthma disappeared shortly after harmonious relations with her husband were established. They have become a happy couple through the elimination of grudges and emotional blackmail. The wife said, "We tossed a coin about the house in the country. My husband lost, but he is a good sport and he loves the new home."

No Need For Third Mistake

Recently a teacher said to me, "I have had three husbands and all three have been passive, submissive, and dependent on me to make all decisions and govern everything. Why do I attract them?" I asked her whether she had known that her first husband was the effeminate type and she replied, "Of course not; had I known I wouldn't have married him." Apparently she had not learned anything from the first mistake. The trouble was with her own personality make-up. She was very masculine, domineering, and unconsciously wanted someone who would be submissive and passive so that she could play the dominant role. All this was unconscious motivation, and her subconscious picture attracted to her what she wanted. She had to learn to *break the pattern by adopting the right prayer process.*

Getting What We Want

We do not get what we want. We attract that which we are, and we are that which we feel ourselves to be. We have to build into our mentality that which we want; in other words, we have to establish the mental equivalent in our mind; then results follow.

Her Ideal Picture

This woman learned a simple truth: When you believe you can *have* the man you idealize, it is done unto you as you believe. The following is the specific prayer she used to break the old subconscious pattern and attract to her the ideal mate: "I am building into my mentality the type of man I deeply desire. The man I attract for a husband is strong, powerful, loving, harmonious, and kind. He is spiritually minded, very masculine, successful, honest, loyal, and faithful. He finds love and happiness with me. I love to follow where he leads. He wants me, and I want him. I have these qualities to offer to a man: I am honest, sincere, loving, and kind. I have wonderful gifts to offer him; they are peace, good will, a joyous heart, and a healthy body. He offers me the same; it is mutual. I give and I receive. Divine Intelligence knows where this man is and the deeper wisdom of my subconscious mind is now bringing us together in its own way, and we recognize each other immediately. I release this request to the Infinite Intelligence within which knows what I want and how to bring it to pass. I give thanks for the perfect answer."

She prayed in the above manner night and morning, affirming these truths and knowing that through frequent occupation of the mind she would reach the mental equivalent of that which she sought.

The Joy Of The Answered Prayer

Several months went by. She had a great number of dates and social engagements, none of which was agreeable to her. When she was about to question, waver, doubt, and vacillate, she reminded herself that the Infinite Intelligence was bringing it to pass in its own way and that there was nothing to be concerned about. Her final decree in her divorce proceedings was granted, which brought her a great sense of release and mental freedom. Shortly afterward she went to work as a receptionist in a doctor's office. She told me that the minute she saw this physician she knew he was the man she was praying about. Apparently he knew it too, because he proposed to her the first week she was in the office, and they are ideally happy. This physician was not the passive or submissive type, but was a real man, a former football player, an outstanding athlete, and was a deeply spiritual man, though he was completely devoid of any creedal or denominational affiliations or attachments. She got what she wanted because she claimed it mentally until she reached the point of saturation. In other words, she mentally and emotionally united with her idea, and it became part of her in the same way that an apple becomes a part of her blood stream.

Should I Get A Divorce?

Divorce is an individual problem; it cannot be generalized. In some cases, of course, there never should have been a marriage. In some cases, divorce is not the solution, no more so than marriage is the solution for a lonely man. Divorce may be right for one person and wrong for another. A divorced woman may be far more sincere and noble than many of her married sisters who perhaps are living a lie.

For example, I once talked with a woman whose husband was a dope fiend, an ex-convict, a wife beater, and a non-provider. She had been told it was wrong to get a divorce. I explained to her that marriage is of the heart. If two hearts blend harmoniously, lovingly, and sincerely, that is God or Love joining two people in a holy covenant or marriage. The pure action of the heart is love, and God is Love. Marriage for any other reason or by any other motivation is a lie, a farce, and a masquerade.

Following this explanation, she knew what to do. She knew in her heart that there is no Law of God which compelled her to be browbeaten, intimidated, and beaten because someone said, "I pronounce you man and wife." If you are in doubt as to what to do, ask for guidance, knowing that Infinite Intelligence will respond to you. Follow the lead that comes in the silence of your soul. It speaks to you in peace.

Drifting Into Divorce

Recently a young couple married for only a few months were seeking a divorce. I discovered that the young man had a constant fear that his wife would leave him. He expected rejection, and he believed that she would be unfaithful. These thoughts haunted his mind and became an obsession with him. His mental attitude was one of separation and suspicion. She felt unresponsive to him; it was his own feeling or atmosphere of loss and separation operating through them. This brought about a condition or action in accordance with the mental pattern behind it. There is a law of action and reaction, or cause and effect. The thought is the action, and the response of the subconscious mind is the reaction. His wife left home and asked for a divorce, which is what he feared and believed she would do.

Where Divorce Takes Place

Divorce takes place first in the mind; the legal proceedings follow later. Each one was cohabitating with resentment, fear, suspicion, and discouragement in the mind; these attitudes weaken, exhaust, and debilitate the whole being. They learned that hate divides and that love unites. They began to realize what they had been doing with their minds. Neither one of them knew the law of mental action and they were misusing their minds and bringing on chaos and misery. These two people went back together at my suggestion and experimented with prayer therapy. They began to radiate love, peace, and good will to each other. Each one practiced seeing the God in the other, and they alternated in the reading of the Psalms every night. Their marriage is growing more blessed every day.

Honor Thy Father And Thy Mother

Boys need a father or a father-image, and the image must be vital, strong, and vigorous. The Bible says, *Quit you like men, Be strong.*

Mothers should put fathers back as head of the house. The father must discipline the boy and see that he obeys. The father is a symbol of authority to the child. The child who honors and respects his father and mother, too, will automatically respect his employer, his professor, the policeman, the laws of his country, and his flag. The wife must never override or undermine the father, as this lowers the authority of the father in the eyes of the child. Mothers should cease practicing "smother love" or over-indulging their children. Fathers should take an interest in their son's activities, play games with them, and pray with them.

The Father Is A Hero

The father is looked upon as a hero by the young boy, and the child wants to imitate him. When the father takes no interest in him and spends his time drinking, golfing on Sundays, or on weekends with other women, the feminization of the boy by his sisters and mother is facilitated. Do not let your son be denied masculine behavior patterns. If his father is dead, get him to associate with an uncle, a relative, or some spiritually-minded man in the neighborhood. The rabbi, priest, or minister will always be glad to take an interest in him and oversee his reactions and moods. His teacher will do the same thing. If you have been divorced, you can attract a wonderful man who will love your son as though he were his own. His father, in that respect, will be the man who impresses him with the great truths of life and nourishes them in his soul. *Honour thy father and thy mother: that thy days may be long upon the land which the Lord thy God giveth thee.*

10

Prayer Casts Out Fear

One of the greatest enemies of man is fear. Prayer, which is faith in God and all things good, casts out fear. Fear is the cloud that hides the sunshine of God's Love. Men have made personal devils of fear of the past, the present, and the future. Fear causes man to fail. It is fear that makes man angry and jittery, causes him to rub others the wrong way, and creates bad human relations. Men fear criticism so much that many of their most beautiful thoughts never see the light of day.

A Bible Prayer

One of the most beautiful and practical prayers in the Bible for the overcoming of fear is this: *The Lord is my light and my salvation; whom shall I fear? the Lord is the strength of my life; of whom shall I be afraid?* PSALM 27:1. This verse might well be indelibly printed in the mind of every man and woman who walks the earth. Contemplate for a moment what it says. It postulates clearly that the Living Presence of God is within you. *Know ye that the Lord he is God.* PSALM 100:3. Another meaning for the word *Lord* in the Bible is *Law,* meaning your subconscious mind.

Learn the powers of your subconscious mind, and you will have light, salvation, and strength, which means understanding, power, and solutions to all your problems. Master the prayer processes elaborated in this chapter. Your subconscious mind will respond, and you will be free of all fears.

Overcoming That Fear

Emerson said, "Do the thing you fear, and the death of fear is certain."

There was a time when the writer of this chapter was filled with unutterable fear when standing before an audience. The way I overcame it was to appear before the audience; do the thing I was afraid to do, and the death of fear was certain. When you affirm positively that you are going to master your fears, and come to a definite decision in your conscious mind that you are going to overcome, you release the power of the subconscious mind which flows in response to the nature of your thought.

One of our students told me that he was invited to speak at a banquet. He said he was panic stricken at the thought of speaking before a thousand people. He overcame the fear this way: For several nights he sat down in an armchair for about five minutes and said to himself slowly, quietly, and positively, "I am going to master this fear. I am overcoming it now. I speak with poise and confidence. I am relaxed and at ease." He operated a definite law of mind and overcame his fear.

The subconscious mind is amenable to suggestion and controlled by suggestion. When you still your mind and relax, the thoughts of your conscious mind sink down into the subconscious through a process similar to osmosis, whereby fluids separated by a porous membrane intermingle. As these positive seeds or thoughts sink into the subconscious area, they grow after their kind, and you become poised, serene, and calm.

Banishing Stage Fright

A young lady was invited to do an audition. She had been looking forward to the interview. However, on three previous occasions she failed miserably due to stage fright.

Here is the very simple technique which I gave her. Remember this young lady had a very good voice, but she was certain when the time came for her to sing that she would be seized with stage-fright. The subconscious mind takes your fears as a request, proceeds to manifest them, and bring them into your experience. On three previous auditions she sang wrong notes and finally broke down. The cause, as previously outlined, was an involuntary auto-suggestion; *i.e.*, a silent fearthought emotionalized and subjectified.

She overcame it by the following technique. Three times a day she isolated herself in a room. She sat down comfortably in an armchair, relaxed her body, and closed her eyes. She stilled the mind and body as best she could. Physical inertia favors mental passivity, and renders the mind more receptive to suggestion. She counteracted the fear suggestion by its converse, saying to herself, "I sing beautifully, I am poised, serene, confident, and calm." She repeated this statement slowly, quietly, and with feeling from five to ten times at each sitting. She had three such "sittings" every day and one immediately prior to sleep. At the end of a week she was completely poised and confident, and gave a remarkable, wonderful audition. Carry out the above procedure with assurance and conviction, and the death of fear is certain.

Can't Remember The Answer

Occasionally young men from the local university come to see me, and also school teachers, who seem to suffer from suggestive amnesia at examinations. The complaint is always the same—"I know the answers after the examination is over, but I can't remember the answers during the examination."

The idea which realizes itself is the one to which we invariably give concentrated attention. I find that each one is obsessed with the idea of failure. fear is behind the temporary amnesia and is the cause of the whole experience.

One young medical student was the most brilliant in his class; yet he found himself failing to answer simple questions at the time of written or oral examinations. I explained to him that the reason was he had been worrying and fearful for several days previous to the examination; these constant negative thoughts became charged with fear. Thoughts enveloped in the powerful emotions of fear are realized in the subconscious mind. In other words, this young man was requesting his subconscious mind to see to it that he failed, and that is exactly what it did. On the day of the examination he found himself stricken with what is called in psychological circles "suggestive amnesia."

A French psychologist named Baudouin said, "What we have to work for in overcoming fear is education of the imagination."

Here is how the young man overcame his fear. He learned that his subconscious mind was the storehouse of memory, and had a perfect record of all that he had heard and read during his medical training. Moreover, he learned that the subconscious mind was responsive and reciprocal; the way to be en rapport with it was to be relaxed, peaceful, and confident.

Every night and morning he began to imagine his mother congratulating him on his wonderful record. He would hold an imaginary letter from her in his hand and read congratulatory words. He would also feel the letter in his hand. As he began to contemplate the happy result, he called forth a corresponding or reciprocal response or reaction in himself. The all-wise and omnipotent power of the subconscious took over, dictated, and directed his conscious mind accordingly. He imagined the end. When he imagined and felt the end, he willed the means to the realization of the end. Following this procedure he had no trouble passing subsequent examinations. In other words, the subjective wisdom took over, compelling him to give an excellent account of himself. The law of the subconscious mind is compulsion.

Shadows In The Mind

There are many people who are afraid to go into an elevator, climb mountains, or even swim in the water. It may well be that the individual had unpleasant experiences in the water in his youth, such as having been thrown forcibly into the water without being able to swim.

I had an experience when I was about ten years of age. I fell accidentally into a pool and went down three times. I can still remember the dark water engulfing my head, and my gasping for air until another boy pulled me out at the last moment. This experience sank into my subconscious mind; for years I feared the water.

An elderly psychologist said to me, "Go down to the swimming pool, look at the water, and say out loud in strong tones, 'I am going to master you, I can dominate you;' then go into the water, take lessons, and overcome it." This I did. I learned that when you do the thing you are afraid to do, fear disappears.

It was only a shadow in my mind. When I assumed a new attitude of mind, the omnipotent power of the subconscious responded, giving me strength, faith, and confidence, enabling me to overcome my fear. I used the subconscious mind to the point where it began to use me.

Following is a process and technique for overcoming fear which I teach from the platform—it works like a charm. Try it! Suppose you are afraid of the water, or a mountain, an interview, an audition, or you fear closed places. If afraid of swimming, begin now to sit still for five or ten minutes, for three or four times a day, and imagine you are swimming. Actually you are swimming in your mind; it is a subjective experience. Mentally you have projected yourself into the water. You feel the chill of the water and the movement of your arms and legs. It is all real, vivid, and a joyous activity of the mind. It is not idle day dreaming, for you know that what you are subjectively experiencing in your imagination will be developed in your subconscious mind; then you will be compelled to express the image and likeness of the picture you impressed on your deeper mind; this is the law of the subconscious.

As you continue to discipline your mind this way, you are mentally immersed in the water and happy in it; consequently the fear passes, and you will enter the water physically. I might say you will be compelled to give a good performance. You have consciously called upon the wonderful power of your subconscious mind which is all wise and powerful; this power controls you and governs you according to the nature of your call or request.

No Boogie Man

The president of a large organization told me that when he was a salesman, he used to walk around the block five or six times before he called on a customer. The sales manager came along one day and said to him, "Don't be afraid of the boogie man behind the door, there is no boogie man; it's a false belief."

The manager told him that whenever he looked at his own fears he stared them in the face and stood up to them looking them straight in the eye; then they faded and shrank into insignificance.

Go out now and face that thing you are afraid of. If you are afraid to take a new position, take it. Say to yourself, "I can accomplish; I will succeed!" You will find a corresponding emotion or feeling generated by your subconscious. You will induce the mood or feeling of confidence, faith in yourself, and the joy of accomplishment. Fear is a thought in your mind, but confidence is a far more powerful thought; it fills your mind with a positive, constructive feeling and drives out fear.

Normal And Abnormal Fear

A chaplain told me of one of his experiences in the second World War. He had to parachute from a damaged plane and land in a jungle. He said he was frightened, but he knew there were two kinds of fear, normal and abnormal. Normal fear is good; it is the law of self-preservation. It is the subconscious mind telling you something must be done. It is sort of an alarm system that tells you to get out of the way of an oncoming car.

The chaplain said, "I began to talk to myself, saying, 'John, you can't surrender to your fear; your fear is a desire for safety or security, for a way out.'"

He said that he knew there was a subjective intelligence which led the birds to their food and told them where to go in summer and winter. He began to claim, "Infinite Intelligence which guides the planets in their course is now leading and guiding me out of this jungle."

He kept saying this out loud to himself for ten minutes or more. "Then," he added, "something began to stir inside me, a mood of confidence began to seize me, and I began to walk. After a few days I came out miraculously, and was picked up by a rescue plane."

His changed mental attitude saved him. His confidence and trust in the subjective wisdom and power within him was the solution to his problem. He said, "Had I begun to bemoan my fate and indulge my fears,

I would have succumbed to the monster fear, and probably have died of fear and starvation."

Whenever fear comes, go to the opposite immediately in your mind. To indulge in fear thoughts constantly and to engage your mind constantly with negative thoughts result in abnormal fear, obsessions, and complexes. To engage the mind with all the difficulties of your problem will only instill more fear until it assumes a size of catastrophic proportions. Finally there comes a sense of panic and terror, weakening and sickening you. You can overcome fear of this nature when you know that the power of your subconscious can always change the objective conditions. Go within, claim and feel your good—the solution. Know there is an Infinite Intelligence which responds and reacts to your thought and feeling.

Imagine the end; feel the thrill of victory. What you subjectively feel and imagine as true is the inner evidence of what will take place objectively. Your subconscious can free you. When fear thoughts come, contemplate the solution, the happy ending. Never fight negative or fearful thoughts. Always turn on the lamp of love, peace, and confidence within you. Most of our fears are imaginary.

The Thing He Feared Did Not Exist

The general manager of an organization told me that for three years he feared he would lose his position. He was always imagining failure. The thing he feared did not exist, save as a morbid, anxious thought in his own mind. His vivid imagination dramatized the loss of his job until he became nervous and neurotic. Finally he lost his position; he was asked to resign.

Actually he dismissed himself. His constant, negative imagery and fear suggestions to his subconscious mind caused the latter to respond and react accordingly. It made him make mistakes and foolish decisions which resulted in his failure as a general manager. The thing this man feared did not exist. His dismissal would never have happened had he immediately moved to the opposite in his mind.

No thought or concept, constructive or negative, can ever manifest except we emotionalize such concepts. The thoughts, concepts, and ideas have to penetrate the subconscious before they can affect us for good or evil.

If you look back in your life, you will agree with the writer that most of your fears, worries, and anxieties never came to pass. The reason for this was that you did not retain them long enough; likewise, you did not charge them with a deep emotion. The general secret of banishing fear is to constantly fill your mind with constructive and positive thoughts. Fill the mind with thoughts of love, peace, and harmony. Give attention to your goal, ideal, the positives, the things you wish to experience in life. As you do this, an inner invisible movement of your subconscious mind will take place, changing your world into the likeness of your inner imagery and contemplation.

Acquiring Inner Peace

During a recent round the world lecture tour, I had a two-hour conversation with a prominent government official. He had a deep sense of inner peace and serenity. He said that all the abuse he receives politically from newspapers and the opposition party never disturbs him. His practice is to sit still for fifteen minutes in the morning and realize that in the center of himself is a deep, still ocean of peace. Meditating in this way, he generates tremendous power which overcomes all manner of difficulties and fear.

Some months ago, a colleague called him at midnight and told him that a group were plotting against him. This is what he said to his colleague, "I am going to sleep now in perfect peace. You can discuss it with me at ten A.M. tomorrow."

Notice how calm he was, how cool, how peaceful! He didn't start getting excited, tearing his hair, or wringing his hands. At his center he found the still water, an inner peace, and there was a great calm.

Your mind is composed of two areas, the conscious mind where we reason, and the great unconscious or subconscious depths which somewhat resemble the ocean into which many forgotten fears and false beliefs are lodged.

Unknown Fears

I met a man who came to my hotel in New Delhi, India, for consultation. He was from the British Isles. He had acute sinusitis, a deep sense of grief, and was haunted by unknown fears. I found in talking to him that he had hated his father for many years, because the father had bequeathed all his estate to his brother. This hatred developed a deep sense of guilt in his subconscious mind; because of this guilt he had a deep, hidden fear of being punished; this complex expressed itself as migraine and sinusitis in his body.

Fear means pain. Love and good will mean peace and health. The fear and guilt which this man had were expressed as disease, or lack of ease and peace.

The mucous membranes of his nose were always inflamed.

This young man realized that his whole trouble was caused by his own sense of guilt, self-condemnation, and hatred. His father had long since passed on to a higher dimension of life. Actually he was poisoning himself through hatred. He began to forgive himself. *To forgive* is to give something for. He practiced saying, "I completely forgive my father. He did what he believed right according to his light. I release him. I wish him peace, harmony, and joy. I am sincere, I mean it."

Then he cried for a long time. That was good. He lanced the psychic wound, and all the psychic pus came forth. His sinusitis disappeared. I have had a letter from him saying that the migraine attacks have ceased altogether. The fear of punishment which was lurking in his subconscious mind has now disappeared.

Use this perfect formula for casting out fear. "I sought the Lord, and He heard me, and delivered me from all my fears." The *Lord* is an ancient word meaning your subconscious mind.

Learn the powers of your subconscious, how it works and functions. Master the techniques given you in this chapter. Put them into practice now—today! Your subconscious will respond, and you will be free of all fears.

"I sought the Lord, and He heard me, and delivered me from all my fears."

The Lord is my light and my salvation; whom shall I fear? the Lord is the strength of my life; of whom shall I be afraid?   PSALM 27:1.

11

How to Pray and Stay Young
In Spirit Forever

During the many years of my public life, I have had occasion to study the biographies of the famous men and women who have continued their productive activities into the years well beyond the normal span of life, some of them achieving their greatness in old age. At the same time it has been my privilege to meet and know countless individuals of no prominence who in their lesser sphere belonged to those hardy mortals who have proved that old age of itself does not destroy the creative powers of the mind and body.

A few months ago I called on an old friend in London who was very ill. He was over eighty and obviously yielding to his advancing years. Our conversation revealed his sense of frustration, his physical weakness—almost lifelessness. His cry was that he was useless and that no one wanted him. With an expression of hopelessness he betrayed his false philosophy. "We are born, grow up, become old, good-for-nothing, and that's the end." This mental attitude of futility and worthlessness was the chief reason for his sickness. He was looking forward only to senescence, and after that—nothing. Indeed, he had grown old in his thought life.

Age Is The Dawn Of Wisdom

Unfortunately many people have the same attitude as this man. They are afraid of what they term old age, the end, and extinction which really means that they are afraid of Life; yet Life is endless. *Wisdom teaches that age is not the flight of years, but age is the dawn of wisdom.* Spirit in man was never born and can never die. Spirit is God, and God has no beginning or end. Man's body is really the garment God wears when He takes the form of man. In order to manifest Itself, Spirit needs a form. Man's body is the instrument through which the Spirit functions on this plane. The Spirit and the body are not separate; man's body is Spirit or Life reduced to the point of visibility. Matter and Spirit are not different—they are the same.

Spirit is the highest degree of matter, and matter is the lowest degree of Spirit. Man will always have a body. When he leaves this plane, he will put on a fourth-dimensional body, and so on to infinity; for there is no end to the glory which is man's.

Life is progression; the journey is a constant unfoldment of our Divinity. All formed things in the universe are gradually returning to the formless life, and the formless life is forever taking form. Anything that has a beginning has an end. Our body had a beginning; it will again return to the formless primordial substance, and we will put on a new body for every end is a beginning.

Welcoming The Change

Old age is not a tragic occurrence. What we call the aging process is change. It is to be welcomed joyfully and gladly as each phase of human life is a step forward on the path which has no end. Man has powers which transcend his bodily powers; he has senses which transcend his five physical senses. Scientists today are finding positive, indisputable evidence that something conscious in man can leave his present body and travel thousands of miles to see, hear, touch, and speak to people even though his physical body is on a couch thousands of miles away. Man's life is spiritual and eternal; he need never grow old for Spirit or Life cannot grow old. Life is self-renewing, eternal, and indestructible. God is Life, and Life is the reality of all men. The evidence of the immortality of man is overwhelming. The scientist cannot see an electron with his eyes, yet he accepts it as a scientific fact because it is the only valid conclusion which coincides with his other experimental evidence. We cannot see God or Life; however we know we are alive. Life is, and we are here to express It in all Its Beauty and Glory.

Mind And Spirit Do Not Grow Old

The Bible says, *This is life eternal, that they might know Thee the only true God.* John 17:3. The man who thinks or believes that the earthly cycle of birth, adolescence, youth, maturity, and old age is all there is to life, is indeed to be pitied; such a man has no anchor, no hope, no vision, and to him life has no meaning. This type of belief brings frustration, stagnation, cynicism, and a sense of hopelessness resulting in neurosis and mental aberrations of all kinds. If you can't play a fast game of tennis or swim as fast as your son, or if your body has slowed down, or you walk with a slow step, remember Spirit is always clothing Itself anew. What men call death is but a journey to a new city in another mansion of our Father's house.

I say to men and women in my lectures that they should accept what we call old age gracefully. Age has its own glory, beauty, and wisdom which belong to it. Love, beauty, peace, joy, happiness, wisdom, good will, and understanding—these qualities never grow old and never die. Emerson said, "We do not count a man's years until he has nothing else to count." Your character, the quality of your mind, your faith, and convictions are not subject to decay.

Love, Peace, Zeal, and Joy Have No Age

I met a surgeon in England who operates every morning, visits patients in the afternoons, and writes in the evening. He is young at 84, full of life, zeal, enthusiasm, love, and good will. He has not surrendered to advancing years; he knows that he is immortal. He said to me, "If I should pass on tomorrow, I would be operating on people in the next dimension, not with a surgeon's scalpel, but with mental and spiritual surgery."

Our own President Herbert Hoover is very active and performing monumental work on behalf of the government at the age of eighty-three. He is healthy, happy, vigorous, and full of life and enthusiasm. I have listened to him speak over the radio; his mind is clear and decisive. I believe his mental acumen and sagacity are much greater now than when he was forty. He finds life interesting and fascinating. I read recently that he spends all the time available in writing a biography of former President Woodrow Wilson. Mr. Hoover is a very religious man with a full faith in God, life, and the universe. He was subjected to a barrage of criticism and condemnation in the years of the depression, but he weathered the storm and did not grow old in hatred, resentment, ill will, and bitterness. On the contrary he went into the silence of his soul and communing with the Indwelling God he found the peace which is the power at the heart of God.

The greatest of all shock absorbers and preventatives of discrepitude and mental and physical disorders is peace at the Divine Center within you. Tune in and feel it now. All the barbs of criticism, anger, and hate aimed at you will be absorbed, neutralized, and lost in the great ocean of God's love and peace within you; this is the secret of remaining young forever.

His Mind Active At Ninety-Nine

My father learned the French language at sixty-five and became an authority on it at seventy; he also made a study of Gaelic when he was over sixty and became a famous teacher of the language. He actively assisted my sister in a school of higher education and continued to do so until he passed away at ninety-nine. His mind was as clear at ninety-nine as it was when he was fifty; moreover, his handwriting and his reasoning powers had improved through the years. Cato learned Greek at eighty. Mme. Schumann-Heink reached the pinnacle of her musical success after she became a grandmother.

There is an old saying which has an underlying truth that a man is as old as he feels. You are as old or as young as your thought. Reason it out for yourself. Ask yourself a simple question such as this: "When was my mind born? When will it die? Has mind and spirit a beginning? How could there be an end to that which has no beginning or end?"

Stay Young Forever

Life was never born, and it will never die. Water wets it not, fire burns it not, wind blows it not away. You know these things to be true. How could you say, "I am old, I am useless, I am unwanted." Never in Eternity could you exhaust the glories and beauties that are within you, for Infinity is within you. There is no end to man since there is no end to God. To maintain this concept will keep you forever young, vital, keen, alert, alive, and full of the Light that never grows dim.

Your gray hairs can be a great asset to you; they symbolize wisdom, understanding, forbearance, and strength of character. Many clergymen receive all manner of wonderful offers when they are over sixty; people believe that they know something by that time. One man said to me recently, "The only reason I come to see you is because you have gray hairs; I believe you have been through the mill, and that you are talking from experience." Ministers find it very easy to get a good position at forty-five. A retired priest recently informed me that he has been receiving fabulous offers from many sources; he was seventy. Truth, Love, and Wisdom have no age. It is possible for a boy of twelve years of age who studies the laws of mind and the ways of the spirit to have a greater knowledge of God than his grandfather who refuses to open his mind to the Truths of God.

Your Gray Hairs Are An Asset

Don't ever quit a job and say, "I am retired, I am old, I am finished." That would be stagnation, death, and you would be finished. Some men are old at thirty while others are young at eighty. The mind is the master weaver, the architect, the designer, the sculptor. George Bernard Shaw was quite active at ninety, and the artistic quality of his mind had not relaxed from active duty.

I meet men and women who tell me that some employers almost slam the door in their face when they say that they are over forty. This attitude on the part of these employers is to be considered cold, callous, evil, and completely void of compassion or understanding. The total emphasis seems to be on youth; i.e., you must be under thirty-five to receive consideration. The reasoning behind this is certainly very shallow. If the employer would stop and think, he would realize that the man or woman was not selling his age or gray hair, rather he was willing to give of his talents, his experience, his wisdom gathered through years of experience in the market place of life. Because of practice and application the man's age should be a distinct asset to the organization. His gray hair, if he has any, should stand for greater wisdom, skill, and understanding. A man or woman with emotional and spiritual maturity is a tremendous blessing to any organization. A man should not be asked to resign when he is sixty-five; that is the time of life when he could be most useful in handling personnel problems, making plans for the future, shaping decisions, and guiding in the realm of creative ideas based on his experience and insight into the nature of the business.

Be Your Age

A motion picture writer in Hollywood told me that he had to write scripts which would cater to the twelve-year-old mind. This is a tragic state of affairs if the great masses of people are not expected to have become emotionally and spiritually mature. It means that the emphasis is placed on youth in spite of the fact that youth stands for inexperience, lack of discernment, and hasty judgment.

I am now thinking of a man sixty years of age who is trying frantically to keep young. He swims with young men every Sunday, goes on long hikes, plays tennis, and boasts of his prowess and physical powers saying, "Look, I can keep up with the best of them." He should remember the great truth: *As a man thinketh in his heart, so is he.* Diets, exercise, and games of all kinds will not keep this man young. It is necessary for him to observe that he grows old or remains young in accord with his processes of thinking. The Spirit is conditioned by thought; if his thoughts are constantly on the beautiful, the noble, and the good, he will remain young regardless of his chronological years.

Job said, "The thing which I greatly feared is come upon me." There are many people who fear old age and are uncertain about the future because they anticipate mental and physical deterioration as the years advance. What they think and feel comes to pass. We grow old when we lose interest in life, when we cease to dream, to hunger after new truths, and to search for new worlds to conquer. When the mind is open to new ideas, new interests, and when we raise the curtain and let in the sunshine and inspiration of new truths of God and His universe, we will always be young and vital.

If you are sixty or ninety-nine, realize you have much to give. You can help stabilize, advise, and direct the younger generation; you can give the benefit of your knowledge, your experience, and your wisdom; you can always look ahead for at all times you are gazing into Infinity. You will find that you can never cease to unveil the glories and the wonders of the Infinite One. Veil after veil is lifted, and Its Face becomes revealed as more august and wonderful. Try to learn something new every moment of the day and you will find your mind will always be young.

I was introduced to a man in Bombay who said he was one hundred ten years old; he had the most beautiful face I have ever seen. He seemed transfigured by the radiance of an inner light. There was a rare beauty in his eyes indicating he had grown old in years with gladness and with no indication that his Spirit had dimmed its lights.

You Must Be A Producer

The newspapers are taking cognizance of the fact that the voting population of the elderly in California elections is increasing by leaps and bounds; this means that their voice will be heard in the legislature of the State and also in the halls of Congress. I believe there should be a federal law enacted prohibiting employers from discriminating against men and women because of age. A man of sixty-five may be younger mentally, psychologically, and physically than many men at thirty. It is stupid and ridiculous to tell a man he can't be hired because he is over forty. It is like saying to him that he is ready for the scrap heap or the junk pile. What is a man of forty or over to do? Must he bury his talents and hide his light under a bushel? Men who are deprived and prevented from working because of age must be sustained by government treasuries at county, state, and federal levels; the very organizations who refuse to hire them and benefit from their wisdom and experience will be taxed to support them. This is a form of financial suicide.

Man is here to enjoy the fruit of his labor and is here to be a producer and not be a prisoner of a society which compels him to idleness. Man's body slows down gradually as he advances through the years, but the mind can be much more active, alert, alive, and quickened by the Holy Spirit. Man's mind does not have to grow old. Job said, *Oh that I were as in months past, as in the days when God preserved me; When his candle shined upon my head, and when by his light I walked through darkness; As I was in the days of my youth, when the secret of God was upon my tabernacle.* Job 29:2–3–4.

Secret of Youth

The *secret* which Job speaks of is joy. All of us can capture our youth by stirring up the gift of God within us. Every time we recognize the Spirit within as Lord Omnipotent and reject the power of false beliefs of the world, we are stirring up the gift of God within us. *In Him there is fulness of Joy. The joy of the Lord is my strength.*

The Prayer Of Rejuvenation

To recapture the spirit of youthfulness, feel the Miraculous, Healing, Self-Renewing, Ever-Living God moving through your mind and body. Know that you are inspired, lifted up, rejuvenated, revitalized, and recharged spiritually. You can bubble over with enthusiasm and joy as in the days of your youth for the simple reason that you can always recapture the joyous state mentally and emotionally. The *candle* which shines upon your head is Divine Intelligence which reveals to you everything you need to know and enables you to affirm the presence of your good regardless of appearances. You walk by His Light because you know that as the dawn appears all the shadows will flee away.

Instead of saying, "I am old," say, "I am wise in the ways of God." You are never a failure for you know that "He never faileth." You can always travel in your mind and conquer new fields. Don't let the race mind, corporations, newspapers, or statistics hold a picture before you of old age, declining years, decrepitude, senility, and uselessness. Reject it for it is a lie. You can rise above the race mind and refuse to be hypnotized by such propaganda. Affirm Life—not death. Realize you live forever, and Spirit is your reality. Get a vision of yourself as happy, radiant, successful, serene, and full of the Light of God. If you are retired, get interested in the Bible, especially its inner meaning. Do something you have always wanted to do, study new subjects, investigate new ideas. Then pray as follows: *As the heart panteth after the water brooks, so panteth my soul after thee, O God.* Psalms 42:1.

Retirement—A New Venture

Be sure that your mind never retires. It must be like a parachute which is no good unless it opens up. Be open and receptive to new ideas. I have seen men of sixty-five and seventy retire; they seemed to rot away and in a few months pass on; they obviously felt that life was at an end. Retirement can be a new venture, a new challenge, a new path, the beginning of the fulfillment of a long dream. It is inexpressibly depressing to hear a man say, "What shall I do now that I'm retired?" He is saying in effect, "I am mentally and physically dead. My mind is bankrupt of ideas." All this is a false picture. The real truth is that you can accomplish more at ninety than you did at sixty because each day you are growing in wisdom and understanding of God and His universe through your new studies and interest.

The Fruits Of Old Age

His flesh shall be fresher than a child's: he shall return to the days of his youth. Job 33:25. Realize that you will never have an old mind unless you think you have. Learn to give all allegiance and devotion to the Indwelling God which is Supreme, the only Cause and Power. To give power to the race mind, to senescence, to sickness, to people, to conditions, and to events divides your allegiance and instills conflict and fear. You might be eighty years old chronologically speaking, but if you are cranky, irritable, irascible, petulant, and cantankerous, you are really old regardless of the number of years you have accumulated whether thirty or ninety. Old age permits the contemplation of the Truths of God from the highest standpoint. This brings you to the well of God where you may drink of the waters of life which will keep you forever refreshed and God-intoxicated.

Look forward to a greater degree of spiritual awareness and realize that you are on an endless journey, a series of infinite steps in the ceaseless, tireless, endless, ocean of God's Love; then with the Psalmist you will say, *They shall still bring forth fruit in old age; they shall be fat and flourishing.* Psalms 92:14. *The fruit of the Spirit is love, joy, peace, patience, gentleness, goodness, faith, meekness, temperance: against such there is no law.* Gal. 5:22–23.

You are a son of the Infinite which knows no end and you are a child of Eternity.

12

Making Prayer More Effective

If your mind is to be stilled, it must be sheltered from the physical disturbances of noise and discomfort, from the winds and storms of the emotions, and from the anxieties and tensions of the day.

The ideal stillness achieved by holy men is a goal for most of us. But in some small measure, each time you withdraw into your prayer room, your mind, you can create a tranquil atmosphere sufficient to make your prayers effective.

Your prayers will never be effective until you cease to battle discords, grief, passion, anger, resentment, and the host of petty emotions that fill too many thoughts. The discipline is for you to release your attention from these disturbances and contemplate the Presence and Power of God within you.

Untroubled by distractions, you can begin to think about a clear understanding of such abstractions as beauty, love, peace, and harmony. When you begin to know the nature of harmony, you can begin to project that quality into the affairs and activities of your life.

Key To Praying Effectively

The Bible gives the perfect formula for making prayer more effective. Consider what it says: *Let the words of my mouth, and the meditation of my heart, be acceptable in thy sight, O Lord, my strength, and my redeemer.* PSALMS 19:14. Answers to your prayers will happen in your life when your inner thought and feeling agree with the words of your mouth.

Long Delayed Lawsuit

A friend of mine was involved in a legal battle which had cost him considerable time, legal fees, etc. He was exasperated, bitter, and hostile toward the opposition and his own attorneys. His inner speech which represents his inner, silent, unexpressed thoughts was more or less as follows: "It's hopeless! This has gone for five years, I am being sold down the river. It is useless to go on. I might as well give up." I explained to him that this inner speech was highly destructive and was undoubtedly playing a major role in prolonging the case. Job said, *For the thing which I greatly feared is come upon me.* JOB 3:25.

He changed his inner and outer speech completely when he fully understood what he had been doing to himself. Actually he had been praying against himself. I asked him a single question as follows. "What would you say if I told you this minute that there had been a perfect, harmonious solution reached and the whole matter was concluded?"

He replied, "I would be delighted and eternally grateful. I would feel wonderful knowing that the whole thing was finished."

He agreed from that moment on to see to it that his inner speech would agree with his aim. Regularly and systematically he applied the following prayer which I gave him: "I give thanks for the perfect, harmonious solution which came through the Wisdom of the All-Wise One." He repeated this to himself frequently during the day, and when difficulties, delays, set-backs, arguments, doubt, and fear came to his mind, he would silently affirm the above truth. He ceased completely making all negative statements verbally and also watched his inner speech knowing that his inner speech would always be made manifest. It is what we feel on the inside that is expressed. We can say one thing with the mouth and feel another in our heart; it is what we feel that is reproduced on the screen of space. We must never affirm inwardly what we do not want to experience outwardly. The lips and the heart should agree; when they do, our prayer is answered.

We must watch our inner psychological state. Some people mutter to themselves, are envious, jealous, and seething with anger and hostility. Such a mental attitude is highly destructive and brings chaos, sickness, and lack in its train. You are familiar with the person who justifies himself; he tells himself that he has a perfect right to be angry, to seek revenge, and try to get even. He is playing an old subconscious record which recites all the alibis, excuses, and justification for his inner boiling state. In all probability he does not know that such a mental state causes him to lose psychic energy on a large scale, rendering him inefficient and confused. Man's negative inner speech is usually directed against some person.

How Truth Set Him Free

I talked to a man recently who told me that he had been treated shabbily; how he planned to get even and how hateful he was toward his former employer, etc. This man had ulcers of the stomach as a result of his inner turmoil and irritation. I explained to him that he had been making very destructive impressions of anger and resentment on his subconscious mind which always expresses what is impressed upon it. These destructive emotions must have an outlet and they came forth as ulcers and neurosis in his case.

He reversed his mental processes by releasing his former employer into the boundless ocean of God's Love and wishing for him all the blessings of Heaven. At the same time he filled his mind with the Truths of God by identifying himself with the Infinite Healing Presence, realizing that the Harmony, Peace, and Perfection of the Infinite One were saturating his mind and body, making him every whit whole. These spiritual vibrations permeating his mind were transmitted throughout his entire system, and the cells of his body took on a new spiritual tone resulting in a healing of his discordant condition.

The Subconscious Recording Machine

The Bible says, *If two of you shall agree on earth as touching anything that they shall ask, it shall be done for them of my Father which is in heaven.* Who are these two? It means you and your desire; i.e., if you accept your desire mentally, the subconscious mind will bring it to pass because your conscious and subconscious have agreed or synchronized. The two agreeing represent your thought and feeling, your idea and emotion. If you succeed in emotionalizing the concept, the male and female aspect of your mind have agreed and there will be an issue or mental offspring, namely the answered prayer.

It must be recalled that whatever we accept or feel as true is impregnated in our subconscious mind. The subconscious is the creative medium; its tendency, as Troward points out, is always lifeward. The subconscious controls all your vital organs, is the seat of memory, and the healer of the body. The subconscious is fed by hidden springs and is one with Infinite Intelligence and Infinite Power.

It is very important to give the proper instruction to the subconscious. For example, if a man dwells on obstacles, delays, difficulties, and obstructions to his program, the subconscious will take that as his request and proceed to bring difficulties and disappointments into his experience; hence, feed the subconscious with premises which are true.

What kind of inner talking goes on in you all the time which is not being expressed audibly? It is your inner talking that the subconscious listens to and obeys. Your subconscious records your silent thought and feeling, and it is a very faithful recording machine. It records everything and plays the record to you in the form of experiences, conditions, and events. You do not have to travel psychologically with fear, doubt, anxiety, and anger. There is no law which says that you have to travel with gangsters, assassins, murderers, intruders, and such thieves and robbers in your mind; they rob you of health, happiness, peace, and prosperity, and make you a physical and mental wreck.

You Are The Only Thinker

A woman had a blood pressure of over two hundred accompanied by severe migraine attacks; the cause of all this was destructive inner speech. She felt that someone had not treated her right and she became very negative toward that other person. She justified herself in being hostile and antagonistic toward this other person, allowing this condition to go on for weeks and was in a deep emotional stew. This negative attitude drained force from her bringing about psychological changes in her blood stream. She was ready as she said, to explode with anger. This inner pressure, mounting tensions, and seething hostility was the cause of her high blood pressure or hypertension plus the migraine.

This woman began to practice the wonders of prayer therapy. She realized she had been poisoning herself and that the other woman was in no way responsible for the way she was thinking or feeling about her. She was the only thinker in her universe, and she had been thinking vicious, destructive, malicious thoughts which were poisoning her whole system. She began to comprehend and see that no one could possibly touch her except through her own thought or the movement of her own mind. All she had to do in order to practice the wonders of true spiritual inner speech was to identify with her aim. Her aim was peace, health, happiness, joy, serenity, and tranquillity. She began to identify with God's River of Peace and God's Love flowing through her like a golden yellow river soothing, healing, and restoring her mind and body.

She prayed for fifteen minutes three or four times a day. Her inner thoughts and feelings were as follows: "God is Love, and His Love fills my soul. God is Peace, and His Peace fills my mind and body. God is Perfect Health, and His Health is my Health. God is Joy, and His Joy is my Joy, and I feel wonderful." This kind of prayer therapy which represented her inner thoughts of God and His qualities brought about a complete sense of balance, poise, and harmony to her mind and body. When the thoughts of the other woman came to her mind, she would immediately identify with her aim—God's Peace. She discovered the wonders of real effective prayer where her lips and heart united in identifying with the Eternal Truths of God, thereby rendering her impermeable to the impact of negative ideas and thoughts.

How do you meet people in your mind? That is the acid test for the Truth which sets you free. If you meet them and see the God in them, that is wonderful; then you are practicing the wonders of inner speech from a constructive standpoint because you are identifying with your aim which is God or the good. Ouspensky, author of *New Model of the Universe,* pointed out that your inner speech should always agree with your aim.

How He Got Agreement

A young man had an aim for perfect health; however his conscious mind reminded him that he had been sick with a blood disorder for years. He was full of anxiety, fear, and doubt. His relations kept reminding him that it would take a long time and that he might never be healed. His subconscious was, of course, receiving all these negative impressions, and he could not get a healing. His inner speech had to agree with his aim. In other words, the two phases of his mind had to synchronize and agree. This young man began to talk in a different tone to his subconscious. I told him as he listened carefully and avidly to affirm slowly, quietly, lovingly, and feelingly several times daily as follows: "The Creative Intelligence made my body and is creating my blood now. The Healing Presence knows how to heal and is transforming every cell of my body to God's pattern now. I hear and I see the doctor telling me that I am whole. I have this picture now in my mind, I see him clearly, I hear his voice, and he is saying to me, 'John, you are healed. It is a miracle!' I know this constructive imagery is going down into my subconscious mind where it is being developed and brought to pass. I know my subconscious mind is in touch with the Infinite One, and Its Wisdom and Power are bringing my request to pass in spite of all sensual evidence to the contrary. I feel this, I believe it, and I am now identifying with my aim—perfect health—this is my inner speech morning, noon, and night."

He repeated this prayer ten or fifteen minutes four or five times daily, particularly prior to sleep. Due to habit he found his mind running wild at times, fretting, fussing, worrying, recounting the verdict of others and his previous repeated failings in the healing process. When these thoughts came to his mind, he issued the order, "Stop! I am the master. All thoughts, imagery, and responses must obey me. From now on all my thoughts are on God and His Wonderful Healing Power. This is the way I feed my subconscious, I constantly identify with God, and my inner thought and feeling is 'Thank you, Father.' I do this a hundred times a day or a thousand times, if necessary."

The young man had a healing of the blood condition in three months. His inner speech became the same as it would be if he had already been healed. *Believe that you have it now and you shall receive.* He succeeded by repetition, prayer, and meditation to get his subconscious mind to agree with his desire; then the Creative Power of God responded according to the agreement. *Thy faith hath made thee whole.*

Why Can't I Sell It?

Here is an example of wrong inner speech: A member of our organization was trying to sell a home for three years. She would decree, "I release this beautiful home to Infinite Mind. I know it is sold in Divine Order to the right person at the right price, and I give thanks now that this is so." This was her prayer and there is nothing wrong with it, but she constantly neutralized it by silently saying to herself, "Times are slow, the price is too high, people don't have that kind of money. What's wrong with me? Why can't I sell it?" You can see that she was rendering her prayer null and void.

As a man thinketh in his heart so is he. Her inner speech was very negative and that was the way she really felt about the whole matter; therefore that mental state was manifested for three years. She reversed the procedure and every night and morning she would close her eyes for five or six minutes and imagine the writer congratulating her on her sale. During the day her inner speech was: "I give thanks for the sale of my home. The buyer is prospered and blessed because of this purchase." The repetition of these prayers were impressed on her subconscious mind and made manifest. A week later a man who sat next to her in church the following Sunday bought her home and was very satisfied. She realized you can't go in two directions at the same time.

Let the words of my mouth, and the meditation of my heart, be acceptable in thy sight, O Lord, my strength, and my redeemer. PSALMS 19:14.

13

How Prayer Banishes Grief and Sorrow

Prayer is a great refuge in which to soften the grief and sorrow that trouble us during the various crises and events that shock us. In the communion of prayer we can resolve true values from the many false values we are apt to place upon the things and associations of this world. The most dramatic crisis is usually the problem of death because with a limited vision we become attached to personalities and we are disturbed by the sharp and apparently final separation of death. It takes the quiet thoughts of prayer to help us realize that death is but a transition between two states of the same life, and to readjust our thinking about our various relationships.

What Is So-Called Death?

Thousands of years ago Job asked, "If a man die, shall he live again?" This question has been asked millions of times since then. The truth is there is no death in the sense of oblivion. God is Life and that Life is our Life now. Life, or God, had no beginning and It has no end. Man being Life in manifestation cannot die. The body had a beginning and the body has an end. Actually we are creating new bodies every moment of the day. Man's body is the vehicle for the expression of life. When the vehicle or body is no longer a fit instrument, it is laid aside. Spirit then clothes Itself in a new body.

Death Is A Beginning

Life is a progression. The journey is from glory to glory; man goes onward, upward, and Godward. Where something ends, something else begins. Usually we admit renewal, resurrection, and fruition processes in the seasons, birds, flowers, and insect life, but when it comes to man, we are struck numb and dumb with fear. We are timid about taking the position that death and birth are but the two sides of the shield of life and should not be feared. Basically it is Life in the process of changing. Something old given up for something new is the transaction consummated in the so-called death process.

There Are No Dead

And this is life eternal, that they might know thee the only true God. JOHN 17:3. To know or to acquaint yourself with the fact that God is the Life of you, the reality of you, is to know that you are immortal, which means the continuity and on-going of your individual life forever expanding into higher mansions of our Father's house. We have our entire being in the Universal Mind of God; this is where all things exist, and whatever abides in the mind of God will never cease to be. A rose that blooms once blooms forever. You are immortal because God is immortal.

When Death Takes Her Boys

One of the greatest tests of character and faith in God and in immortality is to lose loved ones through what man calls death. I chatted with a woman on a recent polar flight to Europe. She told me that she had lost two sons in the war, one was nineteen and the other twenty years of age. The news of their transition was an agonizing mental blow at first, but she added that she quickly regained her composure by quietly affirming to herself, "He is not a God of the dead but of the living, for in His sight all are alive."

She looked at me with a rare radiance in her eyes as she said, "Do you know what I felt?" Her words came slowly and with majestic calm. "Suddenly I felt a wave of inner peace come into my heart and all sense of grief disappeared. I knew and felt that they were alive and I could sense their presence and kindly touch. It was a wonderful experience."

A New Birthday

This woman said that her boys had been very religious, full of love, joy, and vitality, and she continued, "I know God is just and God is good, and I realize that while I miss them, at the same time they are building another home for themselves in the next dimension where they have new bodies and new tasks to accomplish. I asked myself, 'How can I help them?' The answer came quickly: 'Pray for them!' I prayed and reasoned as follows: 'My boys were loaned to me from God, the Source of all Life and the Giver of all gifts. I knew I could not have my boys forever and that some day they would leave me, get married, perhaps go to foreign lands, or move to another city. I loved them while they were with me, I gave them everything I could in the way of love, faith, confidence, and trust in God. My mission now is to help them build a new home, and I radiate love, peace, and joy to them. God's Light, Love, Truth, and Beauty flow through them. His peace fills their souls. I rejoice in their onward journey, for Life is progression. Whenever I think of them I say, 'God is with them and all is well.'"

The above prayer which she repeated several times a day for a few weeks brought a complete sense of peace and tranquillity to this woman. She helped her sons through her prayers, and she helped herself also. *There are bodies celestial and bodies terrestrial; so also is the resurrection of the dead.* I COR. 15:40.

The Oil Of Joy For Mourning

To give the oil of joy for mourning is interpreted this way: We must teach all men that they should never grieve or mourn for loved ones. By radiating the qualities of love, peace, and joy to the loved one who has passed over to the next dimension, we are praying for the loved one in the right manner. We are lifting the other up in consciousness. This is truly giving the "oil of joy for mourning." We rejoice in his new birthday, knowing the Presence of God is where he is. Where God is there can be no evil. In order to pray for the so-called dead, we realize that the loved ones who have passed on are dwelling in a state of beauty, joy, and love; then we are lifting them up because they feel our prayers, and thereby they are blessed. We make them happy by our sincere prayer. Instead of feeling that they are dead and gone, and that their bodies are where the graves are, by an inner mood let us see them dwelling in a state of indescribable beauty. We must never dwell in the mood or feeling of lack, limitation, or regret.

Out Of The Depths

I knew an actor in New York who received a cable-gram that his wife and three children were killed in India only five or ten minutes before he had to go on the stage. He had to sing, dance, and tell jokes. He said to me, "I forced myself to think of God and His Love; I knew the pendulum of life which had swung to trag-edy and despair in my life had to swing to the oppo-site at once. I began to claim that God would give me strength and power and that I would give the greatest performance of my life. Somehow I knew that is what my wife and children would want; as the tears ran down my cheeks, I remembered God and I claimed He was helping me and wiping away all my tears. I offered a prayer for my loved ones claiming that 'He leadeth them beside the still waters' and His Love was there with them." He said his heart was breaking, but he raised his voice in triumphant song and danced as he had never danced before; the house applauded him again and again. He said it was the greatest thrill of his life. He felt God with him all the way. Out of the depths of his sorrow he forced himself to think of God and His Goodness, and God answered him. He invoked the Power which is the greatest thing we know. The Power miraculously took over, elevated him, and gave him strength. He turned his eyes upward; he looked for a solution. *Out of the depths have I cried unto thee, O Lord. Lord, hear my voice: let thine ears be attentive to the voice of my supplications.* PSALMS 130:1–2.

Loyal To His Ideals

I attended a funeral service recently of a man who died suddenly at fifty years of age. He had an only daughter aged thirteen; his wife had passed on when the girl was born. She said to me, "Daddy always said that death was on-going and before he died he said, 'Pray for me, I shall always pray for you and watch over you.'" I was amazed and delighted to hear her say, "I know Daddy heard every word you said. I saw him clearly; he smiled at me. I know he doesn't want me to mourn, cry, or brood over the grave. He wants me to be happy, joyous, go to college, and learn to become a good physician. I know that would make him so happy. I don't owe Daddy tears or sorrow; I owe him loyalty, love, and devotion to the truths he taught, and to make something of myself."

She had solved the tragedy of so-called death in her heart, and it didn't hurt too much. She had the sense of a Divine Companionship which comforted her plus her spiritual knowledge with the principles of happy and constructive living which are kindness, love, growth, confidence, amiability, a sense of trust in the laws of God and His Love for all his own children.

Like this young girl you can rise above your gloom, discouragement, and misery. Rise above it and redeem it now. Come out of your hole of sorrow, grief, and loneliness by emphasizing in yourself the qualities of love, friendship, confidence, trust, and fruitful activities, plus an intense desire for a heightened capacity to love and give of your talents to the world. As you are projecting these qualities while still continuing in loneliness and sorrow, you are building another house in your mind in which you will dwell shortly—if you faint not and keep on trusting in Him, for *He never faileth*. Endure your present trouble while praying for the future state because of the great joy that is set before you.

There Is No Fear In Death

I have been at the bedside of many men and women during their transition. I have never seen any one of them show any signs of fear. Instinctively and intuitively they feel that they are entering into a larger dimension of life. Thomas Edison was heard to say to his physician before he died, "It is very beautiful over there." All of us have a natural wistfulness regarding the state of our loved ones when they leave this plane of life. We must realize that they are living in another mansion of our Father's House and only separated from us by a higher frequency.

The so-called dead are all about us, and we must cease believing that they are dead and gone. They are alive with the Life of God. Radio and television programs fill the room where you are living though you cannot see or hear them without an instrument. Man is under a hypnotic spell of belief in death, but when he lets the scales of centuries of false beliefs fall from his eyes, he will realize that we have an existence beyond time and space as we know it, and he will see and feel the presence of those whom he now calls "dead."

Release Your Loved Ones

It is unwise to hold on to your loved ones in your thoughts. Be sure to release them through prayer; let them go. We must not hamper or restrict their on-going in any way by gloomy, despondent, and dismal thoughts. They are entitled to your thoughts of joy, peace, and love. Millions of people all over the world intuitively feel and know that their loved ones still live, move, and have their being, and moreover they have had a very definite feeling of the near presence of those whom they dearly loved on this plane. The intuitions, insights, and intimations from your subliminal depths which transcend your intellect are constantly reminding you of the deathlessness and eternality of your loved ones.

The *Book of Revelation* contains a beautiful, inspiring, and magnificent passage which touches on life after death. *Therefore are they before the throne of God, and serve him day and night on his temple: and he that sitteth on the throne shall dwell among them. They shall hunger no more, neither thirst any more, neither shall the sun light on them or any heat, For the Lamb which is in the midst of the throne shall feed them, and shall lead them to fountains of living waters: and God shall wipe away all tears from their eyes.* Realize in your heart that they are fed with wisdom, truth, and beauty; their thirst is always satisfied with inspiration from On High and they are flooded with the Radiance of the Light Limitless.

A Spiritual Adventure

I look on death as a birthday into the fourth dimension where we go from mansion to mansion in an ascending scale. About thirty-six years ago I had a severe illness and was unconscious for about three days. All this time I was outside my body and talked with relatives long since gone from the face of the earth; I recognized them clearly. I knew I had a body but it was a different body which enabled me to go through closed doors, and whenever I thought of any place such as London, Paris, or Belgium where my sister was, I was there instantaneously and could see and hear everything that was going on. I spoke to friends and loved ones in the next dimension, yet I used no language; everybody communicated with everybody else by thought. There were no boundaries. Everything seemed to be alive, and I had no sense of time. I felt free, exalted, and rapturously ecstatic. I saw the doctor come into the room where my body was and heard him say, "I think he is dead." I felt him touching my eyes and testing my responses, and I tried to tell him I was alive, but he didn't seem to know I was there. I touched him and said, "Let me alone, I don't want to come back," but there was no perceptible recognition of my touch or voice. The doctor gave me an injection which seemed to be a heart stimulant of some kind. I was furious as I did not want to come back—it was so beautiful in the transcendent state. I was just beginning to enjoy myself, my new acquaintances, and studies in the next dimension. I was being restored to life, and I felt myself going back into by body like going into a sleeping body. Suddenly everything seemed to pass away and I felt I was in prison. When I awakened, I was suffering from shock, undoubtedly due to the anger expressed in the fourth-dimensional body before it entered its three-dimensional counterpart. As far as I know I had experienced what the world calls death, and according to our sense of time I was unconscious seventy-two hours. When men call us dead, we are merely functioning in a higher dimension of mind.

Where Is The Fourth Dimension?

We are living in the fourth dimension now. Actually we are living in all dimensions because we are living in God Who is Infinite. Your loved ones who have passed on are carrying on their lives right where we are but at a higher frequency or vibration. It is possible to have a fan in your room which oscillates at such a high speed that to you it is invisible. Likewise we can send fifty different voices over a cable, and the reason they do not interfere with each other is due to different frequencies. Radio and television programs do not interrupt or collide with each other due to different wave lengths. We interpenetrate all planes, and our journey is ever onward, upward, and Godward.

> *And so beside the Silent Sea*
> *I wait the muffled oar;*
> *No harm from Him can come to me*
> *On ocean or on shore.*
> *I know not where His islands lift*
> *Their fronded palms in air;*
> *I only know I cannot drift*
> *Beyond His love and care.*
> WHITTIER

> *Our birth is but a sleeping and a forgetting;*
> *The Soul that rises with us, our life's star,*
> *Hath had elsewhere its setting*
> *And cometh from afar;*
> *Not in entire forgetfulness,*
> *And not in utter nakedness,*
> *But trailing clouds of glory do we come*
> *From God, Who is our home.*
> WORDSWORTH

Near shady wall a rose once grew,
Budded and blossomed in God's free light
Watered and fed by morning dew,
Shedding its sweetness day and night
As it grew and blossomed fair and tall,
Slowly rising to loftier height,
It came to a crevice in the wall,
Thru' which there shone a beam of light.
Onward it crept with added strength
With never a thought of fear or pride,
It followed the light thru' the crevice's length
And unfolded itself on the other side.
The light, the dew, the broadening view
Were found the same as they were before,
And it lost itself in beauties new,
Breathing its fragrance more and more.
Shall claim of death cause us to grieve,
And make our courage faint or fall?
Nay! Let us faith and hope receive,
The rose still grows beyond the wall.
Scattering fragrance far and wide,
Just as it did in days of yore
Just as it did on the other side
Just as it will for evermore.

ANON.

Never the Spirit was born; the
Spirit shall cease to be never;
Never was time it was not; End and
Beginning are dreams!
Birthless and deathless and shapeless
Remaineth the Spirit forever;
Death hath not touched it at all,
Dead though the house of it seems!
Nay, but as one who layeth
His worn-out robes away,
And, taking new ones, sayeth
"These will I wear today!"
So putteth by the Spirit
Lightly its garb of flesh,
And passeth to inherit
A residence afresh.
THE SONG CELESTIAL

About the Author

A native of Ireland who resettled in America, Joseph Murphy, Ph.D., D.D. (1898–1981) was a prolific and widely admired New Thought minister and writer, best known for his metaphysical classic, *The Power of Your Subconscious Mind*, an international bestseller since it first appeared on the self-help scene in 1963. A popular speaker, Murphy lectured on both American coasts and in Europe, Asia, and South Africa. His many books and pamphlets on the auto-suggestive and metaphysical faculties of the human mind have entered multiple editions—some of the most poignant of which appear in this volume. Murphy is considered one of the pioneering voices of affirmative-thinking philosophy.